Sculpting In Rock

Deep Purple 1968-1970

Adrian Jarvis

Sculpting In Rock

Deep Purple 1968-1970

Adrian Jarvis

WP
WYMER
PUBLISHING
Bedford, England

First published in 2022 by Wymer Publishing
Bedford, England www.wymerpublishing.co.uk Tel: 01234 326691
Wymer Publishing is a trading name of Wymer (UK) Ltd

ISBN: 978-1-912782-06-6

Proofread by Laura Shenton
Edited by Jerry Bloom.

Printed and bound in Great Britain by
CMP, Dorset.

A catalogue record for this book is available from the British Library.

Typeset by Andy Bishop / 1016 Sarpsborg
Cover design by 1016 Sarpsborg.

Contents

1
BOXES

O f the many ingredients that make up heavy rock music, undoubtedly the most important is the fuzzbox. Essentially a pre-amp, it is a humble device that, when plugged into an electric instrument, usually a guitar, adds varying degrees of distortion to the sound produced. In technical language, it pushes sound waves 'to the point that they become close to a square wave as opposed to a sine wave"[1]. Got that? The science aside, it is the fuzzbox that turns the pleasant strum of six strings into the growling, chugging, shredding roar of some nightmarish mechanical predator on the hunt. The blues plus fuzzbox equals heavy rock. Rock 'n' roll plus fuzzbox equals, well, also heavy rock. Fuzzbox distortion increases the gravitational field of everything it goes near. Play a chord on a fuzzbox-distorted guitar and something like a clap of thunder will result. Finger pick a fuzzbox-distorted guitar and you will create that other sine qua non of heavy rock music, a riff. There would be no heavy rock without the fuzzbox.

To say that it was invented in the early 1960s would only be partly correct, since the fuzzbox sound seems to have been discovered by accident[2]. The man responsible was rockabilly legend and much-booked session musician

Grady Martin. His bass solo on Marty Robbins' 1961 single 'Don't Worry' inadvertently went through a faulty mixing console[3], to unexpected, but pleasing, effect. Martin himself was supposedly none too keen on it, but was clearly not blind to the commercial implications because he quickly released a whole single based around his innovation entitled, appropriately, 'The Fuzz' (this may be where the term 'fuzzbox' came from).

This was quickly emulated by The Ventures' 'The 2000 Pound Bee'. In this case, the sound was created by a handmade device built by a friend of the band[4]. The ad hoc nature of these early experiments indicates how niche the fuzz effect was at first: it was yet to demonstrate its potential as a creative force.

Surprisingly, this gauntlet was not picked up by those early pioneers. The rather whimsical titles of the two tracks cited suggest that neither was to be taken entirely seriously. Furthermore, neither — they are both instrumentals — actually makes much use of distortion. In both cases, the fuzz guitar is not foregrounded, but used as a layer, providing something like a drone behind tunes played on more conventional instruments. Novel, then, as these efforts were, they evidence little feel for the fuzzbox's artistic possibilities.

That was left to other 60s hit makers, such as The Yardbirds, The Troggs and, pre-eminently, Jimi Hendrix, the man who, almost single-handedly, made the distorted guitar a viable option for the would-be virtuoso. Again, the sounds were not always achieved by the application of dedicated technology: the amplifier vandalism that led to The Kinks' 'You Really Got Me' was not uncommon[5]. When it finally arrived, the first commercially available fuzzbox gloried in the name Maestro FZ-1 Fuzz Tone.

It took some time to catch on. Sales of it were sluggish at best until the release of The Rolling Stones' evergreen classic, '(I Can't Get No) Satisfaction'. In that single three-minute blast of musical brilliance, Keith Richards transformed the way in which distortion could be used. No longer a mere novelty, it suddenly became a vehicle for the catchy, the complex and the delightful. The song simply would not work without its thick overlay of distortion, which was revealed to be more than just a bauble on an otherwise by-the-numbers composition. It had real depth and meaning. Overnight, distortion became an art form in its own right.

By the end of the decade, heavy rock as a genre was well-established, with the likes of Blue Cheer and MC5 in the vanguard. The reliance on the slipped gear grind of fuzzbox distortion led to the coining of the term 'heavy metal' to describe the highest octane iteration of the music, by, it seems, the critic Lester Bangs. He intended it in a pejorative sense[6], but it was quickly taken up by adherents and worn as something of a badge of honour, although the negative connotations have never gone entirely away; many bands protest that they do not belong in the heavy metal box, despite, in some cases, obviously deserving to be right in there.

Any typology of early heavy rock, hard rock or heavy metal (choose your favourite) behemoths is generally founded on a trio of bands from the UK who, arguably, perfected the art of fuzzbox distortion. The first was Led Zeppelin. Some of their riffs are, quite rightly, legendary, but, how far they, as a band, can be described as 'heavy' is questionable, given their penchant for the folky and acoustic. The second was Black Sabbath whose commitment to the cause cannot be doubted. On tracks such as 'Paranoid', 'Iron Man' or just about anything from *Vol 4*, they showcased an apparent aspiration not only to distort, distort and distort again, but to avoid tunes and melodies like they could kill on first hearing. Finally, there was Deep Purple, the group that concerns us here.

The most mercurial of the three, they were pioneers and perfecters of fuzzbox-based music. Indeed, it is my contention that Deep Purple's *In Rock*, is the par excellence example of the fuzzbox album. I am aware that this may be regarded as controversial. A sizeable constituency will vehemently disagree — as is their right. They might point out that *In Rock* is not the best, or most famous, or most widely-recognised, album of its type. They will pull out any number of counter-examples, some legitimate, others less so. They might go so far as to say that *In Rock* does not even qualify as Deep Purple's best album.

That was the received wisdom for the many years during which the band's later release *Machine Head* reigned supreme. For sure, the average Deep Purple gig is dominated by *Machine Head* songs. After all, it is the album that includes the best opener ever — 'Highway Star' — as well as that perennial entry on lists of the world's greatest riffs, 'Smoke on the Water'. Every other song is also without fault: 'Lazy', 'Space Truckin", 'Pictures of Home', the classics just keep coming. A full performance of the album, in sequence, from start to finish, even provided the basis for a concert tour in the 2000s. It is, without any question, a masterpiece. But is it the band's best work?

A good way to gauge these things is to check out YouTube. Videos in which some enthusiastic middle aged guy in a suitable t-shirt ranks Deep Purple's albums are not exactly rare (I say this as a middle aged guy with a large collection of heavy rock related t-shirts). Invariably, it is *In Rock* that finishes at the top of the pile. It might validly be asked why...

I vividly remember my own first encounter with the album. It was the mid-1980s and I was a callow teenager with a collection of Deep Purple material that was far larger in aspiration than in reality. Back then, albums were

10

expensive and, belonging, as I did, to a not very well-off working class family, funds with which to buy them were limited. After much skimping and saving, I had managed to procure a second-hand copy of *Burn*, as well as the one reductively entitled *Deep Purple* (now often referred to as The Third Album), but that was pretty much it. Neither featured the line-up that made *In Rock*.

Beyond that, I had heard some of the band's music at friends' houses, but usually on one of the many compilations on the market at the time. Of course, they included some *In Rock* tracks; almost always 'Speed King', 'Child in Time', the non-album single, 'Black Night', or any combination of the three. As great as these all were, I was to learn that they do not give a true picture of the album as a whole, being among its more well-mannered representatives.

My first opportunity to obtain my own copy came when the band's label, EMI, got together with a collective calling itself Music For Pleasure to re-release parts of its back catalogue in budget form, giving the series the title 'Fame'. Among the acts subjected to this treatment were not only Deep Purple, but Iron Maiden and Whitesnake. It seems a little odd that music that is now regarded with reverence was ever deemed worthy of a bargain basement re-release, but a separate book can — and should — be written about the doldrums that the record industry was in during the mid-80s. It seems that any way to keep a cash cow alive was grabbed with alacrity.

Anyway, thanks to the Fame programme, I was, after a few weeks of hoarding my pennies, able to go into my local branch of W H Smith, hand over a precious two pounds ninety-nine and walk out with a small rectangular cassette box containing *In Rock* gripped tightly in my hand. I got home and slipped the cassette into my portable just-about-stereo machine (a Christmas present from my parents) and pressed 'play'.

The tape of side one whirred a bit, the slight background 'sh' noise of non-Dolby assisted playback kicked in, then, over it, the music started to play...

In silence, I listened.

'Blown away' does not come close. The bass, played by Roger Glover, rumbled away like thunder, the drummer, Ian Paice, was restless and alive with his sticks, singer Ian Gillan's vocals were a mini anthology of screams, shouts, demoniacal laughs and clean, clear notes that sounded like they should have been beyond the range of the human voice.

Then there were the keyboards. Oh, man! The keyboards! They were played by Jon Lord, weren't they? I had to double-check that. Jon Lord: the guy who had composed classical music, who had played harpsichord — harpsichord! — on the album just prior to this one. What was he up to? He sounded like he was taking out his frustrations on his instruments, his amps, his colleagues and quite probably the studio cat. Finally, of course, there was the febrile guitar of the living legend that was — is — Ritchie Blackmore, axe man extraordinaire, blasting out machine gun riffs and howling solos, pulling it all together, bringing the light, the shade, the sheer massive weight and heft.

Powering him and driving him was the fuzzbox. It dragged every other instrument along with it in a storm of dexterity, audacity, levity and creativity. The album was relentless, unstoppable, beginning with a crescendo of industrial noise and ending with a collapse into chaos. Not a second was wasted and it sounds as fresh today as it must have done upon its first release. It is timeless. A bona fide classic. Others who listened to that Fame cassette with me were as amazed by the album as I was. Decades later, I played the album to Russell, a sceptical friend, and he, too, commented on its contemporary feel and raw power.

That Fame cassette was, as it happens, lost; I leant it to my school for use in an assembly about something or other and never saw it again. I did not own the album again until 1995, when an 'anniversary edition' was released. This time, my format of choice was CD, the plastic case of which was emblazoned with the signatures of the band members. This version was greatly expanded. It included the original seven tracks, all remastered, as well as 'Black Night', which, belatedly, was granted a proper home. There were plenty of other new goodies, all adding context and completeness. Topping off the package were remixes of some of the original tracks and, for some reason, interludes of 'studio chat'. Most of the latter were so brief and uninformative that it is difficult to see who, apart from the most obsessive of completists, would want them. I wanted them.

The remixes and remasters largely served to re-emphasise just how unprecedented, how exciting *In Rock* was... As the first release of Deep Purple's definitive 'Mark II' line-up, it represented a clean break with the past, a reboot, if you like... The past, as they say, was prologue.

Except that it was not.

Hindsight is the worst enemy of the historian and much of what you have just read was written with the benefit of hindsight. With hindsight, we tend to put the past into neatly stackable boxes and impose an order upon it that it did not really have. Nowhere can this be seen more starkly than when looking back at the history of Deep Purple. This point was eloquently made by Jon Lord: 'Well you know, a lot of rock 'n' roll 'history' is by its own nature based on the comments that people make to journalists. Especially in the young part of the band before people have written their autobiographies. Sometimes people say things in anger or in exasperation or in fun and it becomes kind of the bible, when in actual fact when you look back and sort it out it isn't quite as black and white as that'[7].

It is true that Gillan and Glover joined the band in 1969, replacing the founding singer and bassist, but no one at that point would have characterised this as the beginning of a new 'mark'. The whole notion of marks came much later; it frankly only makes sense with a remove of time that throws into relief the unstable nature of the band's make up over its career. Neither was *In Rock* the first Gillan/Glover era release. The new members had already performed on a recording of Jon Lord's *Concerto for Group and Orchestra* (of which, more later). They were also featured on a single, a cover of The Derek Lawrence Statement's 'I Am The Preacher', retitled, 'Hallelujah'. These releases were in much the same style as everything produced by the band hitherto. For all that no less a writer than Cameron Crowe would, with, again, the benefit of hindsight, declare it to be, 'the definitive heavy-metal masterwork'[8], *In Rock* was no more than Deep Purple's fifth album — at least, there is no reason to believe that it would have been accepted as possessing any more significance than that when it was first announced.

Moreover, and more intriguingly, it did not come entirely out of the blue. We may be starting with it, but its rightful place is at the end of the narrative. It superficially sounds very different from the Deep Purple releases that preceded it, but it carries some of their DNA and it would be wrong to ignore the influence and contribution of those others, usually unheralded, sometimes nearly forgotten, who built the band that made the album. What can be said of *In Rock* is that it was pivotal, the one piece of work that transformed Deep Purple and sent them off in a whole new direction, but which, for all the hours upon hours of recorded output that they have given us since, they have never been able to repeat.

This book, then, will tell the story of how *In Rock* came about. It will go into the history of the band up to the point of its release, digging for the album's roots — and, for that matter, the roots of everything that came thereafter. Further, it will look at where the different personalities involved came from, the source bands and underlying themes. In that respect, it will explore the raw material from which *In Rock* eventually emerged, the raw material from which, to coin a metaphor, the album was sculpted.

2
TAPES

When Deep Purple convened at London's IBC Studio in October 1969 to begin recording what would become *In Rock*, they already had a reasonably clear idea of what they wished to achieve. Unlike the many great albums that are more-or-less made up entirely in the studio, the gestation of *In Rock* included a rehearsal period that produced several songs, while giving others that had already been honed on stage the chance to edge towards perfection.

The rehearsals had taken place at Hanwell Community Centre, which, as much as it sounds like a bland and uninspiring place, is in fact a rather elegant range of Victorian buildings in West London, comprising a tower, gardens and several large performance spaces. It was the last of these that most appealed to the band, who were intent upon making a good deal of loud noise, without prompting complaints from disgruntled neighbours[1].

It can confidently be asserted that the rehearsals went well. Jon Lord suggested that the lion's share of the credit for this belonged to the new men, Gillan and Glover, who had the effect of catalysing a period of 'experiment and excitement'. This contrasted sharply with the approach taken by the band previously, which, Lord said, involved too much grasping at different styles. Blackmore agreed, saying, 'Ian is better than the other singer and Roger has more ideas than the bass player we had before'[2].

As stolid and conservative-looking as Hanwell Community Centre is, it proved to be the workshop for some ground-breaking music. The extent to which *In Rock* contributed to the development of a genre is open to discussion, but that it took the members of the band forward as artists cannot be seriously contested.

It was, after all, the band's first studio album of entirely original material. It must be said that a trend in the direction of band compositions dominating had already been noticeable on their more recent releases, but, even so, pre-Mark II output had been liberally peppered with covers. That the Hanwell rehearsals were something of a novel experience for the new members has been pointed out by Ian Gillan, who has characterised them as being about writing songs ('from the perspective of being totally inside them and jamming them') rather than what he was more used to — rehearsals being about learning songs[3].

Another innovation from around this time had much to do with how the album would end up sounding, one prompted by Jon Lord's anxiety about where he would fit in moving forward. He was well aware that the band was evolving into a hard rock outfit and that potentially left little space for his talents[4]. As a keyboard player, he would go on to provide all manner of Moog breaks, electric piano solos and the like for Deep Purple and other bands, but, in the late '60s, technological and other constraints meant that, by default, he had a less rich palette with which to paint: he was, essentially, a player of the Hammond Organ. Lovers of jazz and the blues will be very familiar with this instrument's cool, laid-back, sound. As a main part of Deep Purple's earlier work (which Lord himself described as 'prog rock'), it sounded fine, but the rehearsals underlined the need for fresh thinking[5].

Traditionally, the Hammond Organ had been played through Leslie speakers[6], which made the instrument an ideal foil for saxophones, double basses and unaltered electric guitars, but left it high and dry when pitted against a fuzzbox-distorted Fender Stratocaster. Lord's solution was to plug his Hammond into the rock musician's amp of choice, the Marshall; as he put it himself, 'The sound I was getting was not competing with Ritchie. So I said to our roadie can we tap out of the amp in the Hammond and go into the Marshalls instead of the Leslie — and several electric shocks later we had it'[7]. Distortion was the result. In effect, Lord's Hammond had found its own fuzzbox, although this was by no means the end of every problem. As Lord said, the gentlemanly instrument that had been his Hammond underwent a Jekyll and Hyde-like personality change, 'becoming an almost uncontrollable animal'[8]. Marshalled up, it produced noises that took some effort to keep reined in, as much as they suited Deep Purple's new direction. Not for nothing was it given the nickname, 'The Beast'.

As for the recording process, it generally went smoothly. Stories are legion of rock stars filling studios and control rooms with members of their entourage, or of getting serviced by their girlfriends while laying down their vocal tracks, but it is difficult to imagine that much of that sort of thing ever happened at IBC Studios.

Photographs of the place depict an unprepossessing facade more appropriate to a very proper pre-prep school than a den of rock music excess. The no-frills feel carried over into the interior, which was all cavernous, austere spaces and beige fire doors. The control room was well-equipped, but workmanlike. Overall, the impression is of a professional environment in which people went to do a job, not have a party. The main anecdote from the *In Rock* sessions concerns Gillan getting a blowjob in a corridor (possibly from a certain 'Dirty Doreen') only to be interrupted by a gaggle of office workers heading off for their lunch — more 'Carry On' than 'Deep Throat'.

The 'studio chat' tracks on the In Rock anniversary edition tend to confirm the impression of purposefulness: if they are an accurate record, little time was wasted. That said, the album was not belted out in a short burst of activity, but was recorded on and off over a period of six months. This was necessitated by the band's indebtedness from the 'Concerto' project; money earned from gigging was used to fund studio time. IBC was the location for much of the work, but three tracks were recorded at De Lane Lea and one, 'Bloodsucker', came out of the legendary Abbey Road Studio[9]. Again, this proved felicitous in giving the songs a chance to grow into a more considered and mature final form.

The last piece of the sonic jigsaw puzzle that was In Rock was a certain Martin Birch. Soon to become a fixture in Britain's heavy rock scene through producing duties on albums by bands such as Whitesnake, Black Sabbath and Iron Maiden, he was, at the time, still a young techie trying to make his way in a tough business. His role was officially the unglamorous and uncreative one of 'engineer', but that does not begin to describe his impact on the album's sound. Ian Gillan eloquently described his contribution: 'Musically, Martin didn't have to do anything. He wasn't a producer in that sense, but he was an engineer with a new way of thinking. He didn't 'close down' the studio and baffle everything up and reduce it to zero and then rebuild it on the desk, which was the received knowledge at the time. What he did was listen to how a drum kit sounded in a room and then try and reproduce the sound. This was revolutionary thinking, believe it or not. He somehow got it sounding right. He recorded it loud, and to hell with the meters — they were going into the red all over the place'[10].

Loudness was definitely a key feature. *In Rock* is loud even when it is played at a low volume. It just sounds loud in every note and scream. Famously, Deep Purple's later live album *Made In Japan* includes some onstage chat in which Blackmore asks an engineer to make, 'everything louder than everything else'[11]: the phrase could apply to any part on *In Rock*, on which everything is indeed louder than everything else. That is not to say that it lacks subtlety or musicianship. Ian Gillan, speaking to *Melody Maker*, pointed out that loudness is more than just a case of turning up the amps to eleven — mastering it requires skill and judgement: 'Playing loud is a matter of dynamics. A lot of heavy bands just bash away at the same tune all night, often in the same key. But to play loud you have to work out the dynamics well, and know when to play quietly'[12]. It is *In Rock's* triumph that the band managed to balance this equation to perfection: for all of the distortion, overload and all-round mayhem, the songs always sound well-crafted and considered. Nothing is there by accident. Everything makes some kind of artistic statement.

The first track to be recorded was 'Speed King', which saw the light of day on October 18th 1969, having been worked up in the Hanwell rehearsals. Blackmore has claimed that it was based on Hendrix's 'Stone Free', although the connections are relatively loose[13]. Its first live run-outs had taken place as early as August under the provisional title, 'Kneel and Pray'. Recordings of this version exist and they reveal a far less impressive song than that which eventually made it on to *In Rock*. A fairly standard rock 'n' roll number, 'Kneel and Pray' is entertaining enough but lacks the 'wow factor'. It is particularly uninspired lyrically: the self-reference to a 'simple song' is apt! The chorus, moreover, makes no real impact. On 'Speed King' the chorus integrates seamlessly with the music to build tension and excitement, but on 'Kneel and Pray', it is almost an irrelevant throwaway. A studio recording of 'Kneel and Pray' can be found on the band's BBC Sessions release, where it is given the utterly meaningless title, 'Ricochet' — perhaps to downplay the nudge, nudge, wink, wink associations of what it was actually called.

In its final 'Speed King' form, it is a hard rock perennial, bold of riff, surprising of solo and witty of lyric. In many ways, it is the ideal showcase for the band's varied talents. It begins with a huge fuzzbox attack from Blackmore (recorded separately as 'Waffle' on November 4th), before settling down into an organ run from Lord that sounds like nothing so much as a little Sunday morning church music. It is fanciful to say so, but in that first minute or so of the song, a debate that had been raging within the band over the previous months is resolved. There is no further introduction, simply a drum beat, followed by Gillan singing wildly over the crashing main riff. The lyrics are inspired. That the song is about the drug speed is a popular myth, often debunked by members of the band. Gillan has said that it is about 'desperate singing'[14]. To be honest, the lyrics cannot be said to mean much, but by borrowing images and phrases from rock 'n' roll songs of the past ('good golly said little miss Molly', 'tutti frutti', 'Lucille' and the evocative reference to a 'house of blue light' — a 1946 song by Don Raye and Freddie Slack and recorded by both Chuck Berry and Jerry Lee Lewis amongst others), they bring out the poetry of the genre. The central instrumental break is something of a surprise. Everything slows down for a guitar/organ duel that sounds like nothing so much as a jazz improvisation. It ends with a build-up, enhanced by slide guitar and booming bass, until Gillan comes back in with some 'whoops', cheesy villainous laughter and a few post-orgasmic 'ohs'. This was, once upon a time, the band's concert opener; it is difficult to see how they had the energy to do a whole gig having played it.

'Living Wreck' was recorded next, also on the 18th. One of the few songs on the album with lyrics that tell a comprehensible story, humour is the order of the day as a (hopefully) fictional narrator complains about a woman (known widely, we are told, as 'Big G') who joined him for a weekend of, it can be guessed, sexual debauchery, but who only stayed for a single night, having presaged a tumble into bed by taking off her hair and pulling out her teeth. Musically, the tempo is relaxed and anchored by a catchy riff, which does nothing to prevent the Beast from roaming free, filling the gaps with shrieks and howls and sweaty solos. By contrast, Blackmore keeps things mellow with a passage that is dreamy and ambient.

On November 4th, the band recorded the track that would for many years — until the unstoppable rise of 'Smoke on the Water' — be regarded as their masterpiece, the ten-minute mini-symphony that is 'Child in Time'. It starts with some cool reflective organ before Gillan joins in, his voice gentle and small. It does not remain so for long. A succession of soaring 'ahs' and screams drag the band along as the power and volume grow. Gillan tells the story of how this part of the song came about: '[The other band members] never used to listen to me about the key. But the key is too high. Well, sing higher. But it's beyond my range, so, in the end, I just kept going up and up and up.'[15]. When it seems like no human voice could ever go higher, an abrupt fill of marching drums announces the beginning of the long faster, harder, instrumental section. The pace comes down for a reprise of the vocal parts, but this is just a brief interlude ahead of another rush towards the crashing finale. With changing tempos, virtuoso playing and maestro-level singing, the song is thrilling, magnificent and, ultimately, cathartic.

Yet, it was based on a piece of musical larceny. The band never even tried to conceal the fact that the basic organ riff was an almost direct lift from a song called 'Bombay Calling' by the hippyish Americans It's A Beautiful Day. Gillan has spoken of how it happened: '[Someone] said, yes, have you heard that song called 'Bombay Calling'? I said, no. Well, they're an instrumental band, so we played it on a cassette, or something — and it's very fast. And Jon was sitting at the piano and he was going bom, bom, bom. I said, that's just incredible. So I started singing'. Glover adds: 'Lo and behold, a song appeared. Yes, it's borrowed, but it's something that [It's A Beautiful Day] would never have written and something we wouldn't have written without them.'[16]

This will be far from the last time that such borrowing will be mentioned in the context of Deep Purple, or even *In Rock*, but, back then, no one seemed to care too much. Musical cross-fertilisation was accepted as a natural part of the songwriting process, lawyers rarely getting involved. Indeed, It's A Beautiful Day would go on to filch heavily from Deep Purple's own 'Wring That Neck' for a track on one of their later albums[17].

Lyrically, 'Child in Time' is, arguably, Ian Gillan's finest achievement. He has frequently claimed that the song is about the threat of nuclear annihilation[18], but that does not come through as a strong theme. *Melody Maker's* take was that it all added up to 'moralising in too general terms about the State of Things'[19]. This is about right. The descriptions of seeing the difference between 'good and bad' and a blind man taking pot shots at the world and the listener having to wait for the ricochet do not have much of the mushroom cloud about them: there is no specific point of reference. The lyrics are more elusive and poetic. They are of that school of semi-mystical writing that trades more on affect than idea. Nonetheless, they are strangely powerful, even moving. This is partly, of course, because of the way in which they are sung, but, even on a literary level, they have something to say to all of us. Gillan's description of their creation characteristically plays down any artistic pretensions: 'It was just a tune. Sometimes the words just pop out of the air and it did with that one.'[20]. Incidentally, given that the opening lines are 'Sweet child / In time you'll see the line', perhaps the title should include a comma?

In later years, as relations within the band began to deteriorate, 'Child in Time' would become something of a battleground for Gillan and Blackmore's warring egos. The song was a tremendous strain for the singer, so he would request that it be dropped from the set list if he was not feeling on top form. Forearmed with this, the guitarist would choose a suitable place in the running order and begin to play it. The predictable roar from the crowd obliged Gillan to give it his all. It is telling that, at the time of writing, Gillan has not performed the song live for decades. Blackmore has played it with both the renaissance-flavoured Blackmore's Night and the revived Rainbow that did the rounds prior to the pandemic lockdowns.

It says something about the challenges of 'Child in Time' that it was a full three weeks before any more of the album was recorded. When the sessions resumed, they produced, first of all, 'Into the Fire', recorded on 27th November. Little needs to be said about this track. Its title is obviously a kind of warning, being the second half of the phrase 'out of the frying pan and...' Supposedly carrying an anti-drug message, the song is, again, lyrically vague, despite including mentions of 'mandrakes' and 'finger popping'. More interesting is the degree of distortion, which gives the guitar a dirty and ragged feel not always evident elsewhere. The riff is memorable, one reason that the song has been in and out of set lists for much of its life — most recently, gracing live albums from well into the 2000s.

On the same day, the band recorded 'Jam Stew'. Although it did not gain full *In Rock* track status until 1995, this one floated around in various forms during its formative years, cropping up here and there in some unpredictable places.

Basically an instrumental, a version done as part of a BBC session included some impromptu singing by Gillan (demonstrating that it would have made for a very passable vocal number). A later BBC session included a certain 'Grabsplatter', another wordless gallop that was based around a reworking of 'Jam Stew's feverish, urgent main riff.

More weirdly, the tune, retitled 'Bullfrog', appeared again as a main feature of the album called *Green Bullfrog*, recorded in 1970 and released, to general indifference, in 1971. The brainchild of producer Derek Lawrence — a long-time friend of Blackmore and a figure who will crop up again in relation to the early history of Deep Purple — it was the it-is-what-it-is outcome of a project that aimed to get a few rock, pop and blues musicians together to put something — anything — on tape. Blackmore and Ian Paice were Deep Purple's representatives. Others included Tony Ashton (later to work extensively with Paice and Lord), Blackmore's mentor Big Jim Sullivan, Albert Lee and, of all people, Chas Hodges, the man who would go on to be one half of the ridiculously entertaining duo, Chas and Dave. For legal reasons, none of these people's names could be used when publicising the album, so some bizarre pseudonyms were devised (Blackmore, for example, was credited as 'Boots'). The players' true identities were revealed much later, but, by then, the damage had been done; it can be guessed that the inability of Lawrence and his backers to appeal directly to loyal fan bases largely accounted for the project's financial failure.

Blackmore and Paice were back at their day jobs to see in the new decade with Deep Purple, who decamped to De Lane Lea Studios to lay down 'Hard Lovin' Man'. This song is, in many respects, the quintessential *In Rock* track. Its seven whacky, incredible, mind-blowing minutes encompass a pounding riff, a throbbing bass line that simply does not know when to quit, a gloriously discordant organ solo, feedback, tremolo arm madness and lyrics that can only be from the point of view of a man in the act of having sex. Throughout, Lord is at his most out of control, his keyboard sound occasionally degenerating into sheer, ear-splitting, noise. Somewhat surprisingly, the song is one of his favourites, it being, he said, the first time that he was able to bring his onstage 'antics' into the studio. As late as 2009, he said of the recording: 'I still remember the day. I remember the engineer thinking I'd gone bananas and lost the plot'[21]. This anecdote may have nothing to do with the song being dedicated to Martin Birch, who, it can be imagined, was flattered by the association. Strangely, 'Hard Lovin' Man' enjoyed few live outings until the new century, when it became a set staple — with the irony that the men playing it were, by then, way past the age at which their loving stood much chance of being more than usually hard.

It was to be nearly another fortnight before any more work was done on the album and, when it finally was, another false start was the result. Having returned to IBC, the band took thirty-one takes to perfect 'Cry Free'[22] — far more than were needed for any other track. Nevertheless, it was still excluded from the completed album and only appeared as part of a rarities compilation called *Powerhouse* that was released in 1977. It is easy to see why. Conceived as a possible single, the song is an enjoyable enough piece of rock bombast, but lacks a catchy hook — it can be categorically stated that it would not have attained the same degree of success as the single that was eventually decided upon. It also would not quite have fitted on the album. Yes, it has the requisite heaviness and the individual parts are all done as well as might be expected (with Gillan's singing a standout), but it does not quite mesh with the style of the other songs. As a bonus track on the anniversary edition, it is required listening; as part of the original album's golden seven? Not so much.

Another pass at 'Speed King' followed at the end of the month, before De Lane Lea became the venue of choice for a day in March on which 'Flight of the Rat' was given its definitive form. The title is, according to Gillan[23], a variation on 'Flight of the Bumblebee', the 'rat' in question being drugs, although, again, this is somewhat opaque in the lyrics. Occupying that most unenviable position, 'minor classic', this one embodies all of the characteristics of the album of which it is a part, without ever quite getting ahead of the best of the rest. It could be said that it lays down the template for later Deep Purple tentpoles like 'Highway Star' and 'Burn': strong riff; twiddly, baroque, bits that remind the listener that these guys are doing this because they want to, not because they have to; crazy solos that give everyone an opportunity to shine (even Ian Paice gets his moment in the sun); verses that serve mainly to pull everything together. The song is notable for Blackmore playing one solo on the wah-wah pedal — a nod to Deep Purple's past, perhaps. As an entry on the track list, 'Flight of the Rat' is one of the more entertaining, but, nonetheless, it does not seem to have been performed live much, if at all. Calls from fans and even band members to give it another chance in the 2010s came to nothing when rehearsals failed to rescue it from having a dated and irrelevant air. More's the pity, since it would no doubt light up the average gig: it is certainly one of the band's more danceable tunes.

Abbey Road welcomed the band on April 13th. The studio may not have had the aura then that it has today[24], but it must still have been an evocative setting in which to work. The Beatles' last recorded album, released in September '69, was simply named after the studio and undoubtedly raised its profile.

It is a pity, then, that the track recorded was the relatively workaday 'Bloodsucker'. By no means bad and Exhibit A in any charge that the band deserves the 'heavy metal' tag, it fits in well with the rest of the album, but is not a standout. Revived for tours in the 1990s, it is most notable for being one of only two tracks that the band have re-recorded, in this instance for the 1998 *Abandon* album, on which it is inexplicably renamed 'Bludsucker'.

And that was it! The band had their album. There was some shuffling around, of course: not everything made the cut. Blackmore laid out the manifesto for what could and not be included when he bluntly stated, 'If it's not dramatic or exciting, it has no place on this album'[25]. Even 'Living Wreck' was nearly left on the shelf until a re-listen convinced the band that it was quite good after all[26]. Intense conversations must have been had, but, at some point, the final seven were chosen. A musical landmark had come into being.

Unfortunately, the management wanted a single and none of the songs obviously met the requirement[27]. 'Speed King' is catchy enough, but, at nearly six minutes, it was far too long for the taste of the time and, besides, its mid-section tempo changes would have made it a tough sell. The other candidate, 'Cry Free', was also deemed unsuitable. What to do?

The answer was to return to De Lane Lea at the beginning of May to record a single. Inspiration was low, however, and, after much messing around and a few dead ends, the decision was made to suspend work and head off to the local pub[28].

By the time they made it back, the band members were all allegedly rather well-oiled. Blackmore picked up his guitar and, it can be guessed, more to get himself back into the mood than as a serious suggestion, began to play the bass line from Ricky Nelson's 1962 rendition of Gershwin's 'Summertime'. It proved to be enough to get the rest of the band moving and was swiftly developed into a main riff. Blackmore has never been coy about this particular bit of plagiarism; as recently as the 2010s, he could be heard gleefully explaining his inspiration: 'It was not entirely original — I stole it!'[29]. He gave more detail in a 1995 interview: 'I knocked out the Ricky Nelson 'Summertime' bass riff which went bom-bom ba-bom-bom; we did that as a shuffle. Because the top line to Ricky Nelson's 'Summertime' was 'Hey Joe' before 'Hey Joe' came along. 'Summertime' came along in about 1962. Then Jimi came along in '68 and used the top line. So I thought if he can use the top line, we'll take the bass line'[30]. Lord described the process of composition: 'Ritchie said, again, what about that, you know that version of Ricky Nelson's 'Summertime', the Gershwin song? We went, yeah. He said, well, there's a little riff under there, which went dom dom der dom dom dear dom — but it just went round and round. So we played it round and round and it got very quickly very boring. One of us — who knows who — came up with the idea of having a turnaround in it: dom dom der dom dom der dom dom der dom der dom da da — which made it a little less repetitive and boring. And then Ian Paice did one of his magical little things, one of those drum breaks that he used to come up with. What are you doing there, Ian? I have no idea, it just fits. So that was cool. Suddenly, we had a sort of a structure'[31].

The lyrics were deliberately intended to be as banal and incomprehensible as possible, as Glover has said: 'The 'Black Night' name was stolen from a song by [his and Gillan's previous band] Episode Six and then we invented funny rhymes: night, bright, right — whatever came to our minds was all right'[32]. Lord added another question around the name of the song: 'Spelling is important there: we never knew whether it was n-i-g-h-t or k-n-i-g-h-t. So it's either about a chess piece or a particularly cloudy English winter evening'[33].

It is more than a little bemusing that 'Black Night' is always held up as the prime example of the Deep Purple nonsense song, given how many, even on *In Rock*, fit that description. 'Speed King', 'Into the Fire', 'Bloodsucker' and 'Flight of the Rat' are all, to put it mildly, elusive of meaning. 'Child in Time' only gets away with it because of Gillan's constant insistence that it is something to do with the shadow of the bomb.

Still, with a few nips and tucks, a single that would be acceptable to BBC Radio was completed and duly presented to impatient management. Either they were unaware of its blatant lack of originality or simply didn't care and it was readied for release at the same time as the album.

Why *In Rock*? The album obviously does not have a title track — few Deep Purple albums do — so where did the title come from? In fact, it was an attempt to resolve an identity crisis from which the band had suffered since its inception in 1968, to wit, exactly what was their style? More will be said about this later, but it was touched upon in *Melody Maker's* review of Mark II's 'Hallelujah' single, which was positive, but ended with the pertinent observation, 'I haven't a clue which direction they are headed'[34]. It was something the band were all too aware of themselves, Blackmore telling *New Musical Express* in 1969: 'We want to be known in England, so we've come out very much on the commercial side with the new record'[35]. The main problem was that the band's most high profile activity up to that point had been the Lord-led *Concerto for Group and Orchestra* (of which, again, more later), which Blackmore dismissed as a 'gimmick'[36]. The new album needed to distance itself from such experiments before the band became too associated with them. Therefore, it needed to establish in the minds of the public that Deep Purple were not just a group of pop musicians who played along with orchestras, but fuzzbox-wielding innovators. It had to let the world know that they were rockers, and, more than that, forged from, of and in rock[37].

All that remained was to create an eye-catching piece of packaging. Album covers tend to be either much maligned or unduly lauded, but they are a potential purchaser's first point of contact with a band's work and need to be carefully judged. Some have become iconic, although it is not always clear why — is the cover on the Beatles' *Abbey Road* really all that good? Since Paul McCartney could not even be bothered to stub out his cigarette before being photographed, it would seem that the band themselves didn't pay too much attention to it. For *In Rock's* cover the stakes were relatively high. It had to stand out on shop racks, while hinting at changes to both personnel and musical direction.

Previous Deep Purple album covers had been rather hit-and-miss. The first gives the title on top of a hilariously awful picture of the then band members, including a sheepish-looking, bouffant-haired Blackmore. The next, *The Book of Taliesyn*, has a sublime cover: a brilliant piece of pseudo-medieval art, it is easily the best thing about what is, otherwise, an inconsistent album. The third, self-titled album has a rather ho-hum black and white recreation of part of a Hieronymus Bosch painting with a picture of the band members superimposed. Bizarrely, this innocuous concoction was banned from open display in some parts of America, prompting the band's manager Tony Edwards to remark: 'It does seem particularly weird that, in one or two of the more puritanical States, they are taking exception to a painting which has been displayed for so long in one of the great religious centres of the world'[38].

The cover to *In Rock* was based on an idea by Edwards to replace the presidential heads on Mount Rushmore with those of the band's members (one would have thought that this would be the cover to which Americans would take most exception...). Whether it was the plan or not, it laid down a template for all but one of the band's albums prior to their split (in retrospect, hiatus) in 1976, which would feature quirky head shots of the band members[39].

By all accounts, Edwards spent some considerable time sourcing images of Mount Rushmore from the picture libraries of London — it would be the job of minutes in this Internet-enabled age. The design agency Nesbit, Phipps & Froome took over from there, taking photographs of the band and hand pasting them on to the chosen Rushmore picture.

The title lettering was invented by the agency[40]. It was unique to the album and illustrates another interesting point about Deep Purple: their career-long absence of a stable logo. The closest they have come is either the curly design used on the much later live album *Made in Europe* — which was reused on a couple of semi-official compilations as well as on a million pieces of merchandise. Or the slightly irritating 'P inside D' emblem that graced the front cover of the 1980s reunion album, *Perfect Strangers*.

Behind the main picture on the *In Rock* cover is nothing

more than a pale blue fill-in. In some respects, this is the most memorable part of the whole. Certainly, when I think of *In Rock's* cover, I think of it as 'the blue one'.

A gatefold sleeve, the inside was simple and clear: credits, very brief track notes, close-ups of the band and, unusually for the time, lyrics. Given how little the lyrics actually mean, this last present to the fans cannot have added much to the experience. Colourful and direct, the cover did — and continues to do — a good job of distinguishing itself from the vinyl crowd.

Deep Purple In Rock was released on June 5th 1970.

The story does not quite end there. Much will still need to be said about the album's reception and legacy — not to mention how it influenced live performances and future recordings. But any discussion of Deep Purple between 1968 and 1970 will, as a matter of course, reach a significant point with that date in the early summer of a new decade. What remains is to explore the album's archaeology. In order to do so, we need to scrabble around a little in the stony rubble of the history leading up to it: the social, biographical and, above all, musical. As good a place to start as any would be where it all happened, the country from which all of the key players came and which lies behind so many of the lyrics to songs like 'Living Wreck' and 'Flight of the Rat': England. Specifically, post-war England.

3
ROOTS

Tommy Steele: now feted as an all-round entertainer and paradigmatic national treasure, he is an unlikely point of origin for *Deep Purple In Rock*. Yet, he is as good a place to begin as any. The performer of such hits as a strangely jolly 'Singing the Blues' and the bizarre-sounding 'Rock with the Caveman', he was a — maybe the — formative influence on the British *rock 'n' roll* scene in the late 1950s. His soundtrack to the self-effacingly titled film, *The Tommy Steele Story,* was the first British album to reach the top of the UK charts. The key word here is 'British', because, notwithstanding that his singing resembled that of a young Elvis, Steele was always firmly rooted in his home country.

This is important because the Englishness of much of the music that concerns us should not be overlooked and of the three great English heavy rock/metal bands who defined the fuzzbox sound in the late 60s and early 70s, the most English — the most, in that sense, Tommy Steele-like — were Deep Purple. Led Zeppelin primarily adopted American styles (often doing little more than repurposing existing songs), their singer Robert Plant embracing a faux American drawl as he belted out his vocals. Likewise, the Birmingham accent of Black Sabbath's Ozzy Osborne is largely absent from his singing voice. Ian Gillan, by contrast, sounds like an Englishman. His pronunciation retains the flat vowels and understated intonation of English English. On the *Machine Head* track 'Space Truckin", a golden opportunity is presented for him to sing a few clichéd 'come oun's like an American, but, no, he always sticks with 'come on'. He is known for his screams, but they are 'whoops' not 'yee-ha's.

If, indeed, we are to get to the bottom of where *In Rock* came from, the England of the 1960s, the England of Tommy Steele, is a crucial context. It is not too much to say that, back then, it was a country in the middle of massive, almost certainly seismic, and, perhaps, revolutionary, change. When thinking about that time, and that place, we focus on certain landmarks: *Time* Magazine's 'Swinging London' cover, the England team winning the football World Cup, the Beatles' rooftop concert — these were the highlights, but the England from which the personnel who made *In Rock* emerged was a much more complex and ungraspable place than can be summarised so easily.

At the beginning of the 1960s, the country still skulked in the shadow of World War Two. 'Kitchen sink dramas', such as *Saturday Night and Sunday Morning*, *The L-Shaped Room* and *Room at the Top* portrayed England as a bleak, joyless place in which hope was a rare commodity. The black and white cinematography of such films seemed more like realism than part of a filmmaker's technical arsenal. 'Big G' from 'Living Wreck' could comfortably have been a character from one of those films — she would not have made an appearance in anything coming out of America.

While social mobility was not quite as stagnant as it had been for much of history up to that point[1], many routes to financial and social success were still rather exclusive and exclusionary. Music was not one of them. The Rolling Stones would go on to ask, 'what can a poor boy do, except sing for a *rock 'n' roll* band?' — it was a fair question. Most of the musicians who led the 1960s revolution — the great cheering up of England — were from relatively modest working, or lower middle, class backgrounds.

One was a certain Richard Hugh Blackmore. Blackmore was born, although not raised[2], in Weston-Super-Mare in the West of an England at the fag end of World War Two: he entered the world almost exactly a fortnight before Adolf Hitler left it. The best thing that can be said about the place of his birth is that it also produced John Cleese, some years earlier, meaning that two great icons of twentieth century English culture were in the town, as small children, at the same time: it is to be wondered if they ever crossed paths without knowing it. Unlike Cleese, Blackmore was not a great academic and was somewhat directionless at school.

At the age of thirteen, he took up the guitar, perhaps to give himself something to do that he could be really good at. He succeeded. Roger Glover has described Blackmore as someone with an almost supernatural talent for the instrument[3]. Blackmore himself was less certain, explaining that whatever gift he may have had was augmented with an obsessive devotion to practice: 'I really need to sit down and practise a lot... I love practising' he said[4].

Perversely, he has claimed that his first aspiration was to play classical guitar[5], but this quickly died down when he heard that man Tommy Steele on television. Newly galvanized, Blackmore set off on a path that would lead to a career, fame and fortune[6].

His first bands, formed while still at school, gloried in names such as The Electric Vampires and The Dominators (an early sign of the dictatorial tendencies noted by many later band members?). From there, he went on to join

Mike Dee and the Jaywalkers. One of their gigs, at Southall Community Centre was notable for being attended by a young man who was almost exactly Blackmore's contemporary and whose career would go on to follow similar lines — Nick Simper.

Simper's tale is laced with many odd and quirky moments, but perhaps none is more intriguing than the fact that he bought his first electric guitar from a shop owned by Jim Marshall, the man behind the amps that helped to create the hard rock sound — not least by being the means by which Jon Lord's 'Beast' was born.

Simper's biography also includes membership of Johnny Kidd and the (New) Pirates, which put him at the heart of some of the most successful and influential music being produced in Britain at the time.

As for Blackmore, while his early bands achieved a certain amount of local success, it was only during a brief stint with the *rock 'n' roll* eccentric Screaming Lord Sutch that he began to attract any degree of wider notice. Best known to whole generations of British people as the leader and sole candidate of the Official Monster Raving Loony Party (which contested a string of UK general elections between the 1980s and early 2000s) Sutch began as a member of the 1960s generation of musicians that did much to pull the country out of its long post-war depression. His subjects were often controversial, 'Jack The Ripper', for example, being an upbeat party song that seems to celebrate the titular murderer.

The other future Purple stalwart, Jon Douglas Lord, was born in the East Midlands town of Leicester, the unassuming accent of which never left him. He started to learn the piano at the age of five, but earning his living from it was not his first ambition. Instead, at seventeen, he enrolled at the celebrated Central School of Speech and Drama in London, intent upon being an actor[7] — or, intent upon using acting as a way to escape the stiflingly parochial life that he had lived up until that point. He said: 'I could easily see that if I stayed in Leicester I would end up working in a factory or in an office. I became aware when I was eighteen or nineteen that this was not for me. That is why I went to London and entered the drama school'[8].

Following a minor revolution (only the first of many for one of the world's less likely revolutionaries), he broke away with some other students and teachers to form the Drama Centre London, which he left, diploma in hand, in 1964. On the face of it, there is no particular reason why he could not have become a star of stage and screen: tall, slim and handsome, he had all the attributes of a leading man. Later interviews and performances definitely confirmed that he had plenty of presence, but his was a classic case of a person's sideline becoming their main job. Paying the rent by playing piano at bars and as a session musician, he devoted less and less time to acting, which began (pun intended) to play second fiddle to the more lucrative job.

Lord's first professional musical engagement was with the jazz group The Bill Ashton Combo in 1960. Once highly regarded on the British jazz scene, Ashton is now rather obscure — to the extent that his music is not available even on that treasure chest of the obscure, YouTube. This period, however, brought Lord into contact with one of the most important elements that would eventually coalesce into *In Rock* — as Lord himself put it: 'When I first heard the Hammond Organ I was not playing rock music. I was at drama school back then and heard Jimmy Smith playing the Hammond Organ'[9].

The other East Midlander in this story is a certain Ian Anderson Paice. Younger than Blackmore and Lord, his early life was passed in the industrial city of Nottingham. Following a move to Oxfordshire, he took up the drums and soon became good enough to play with his father's big band on Saturday nights[10]. A long-term effect of this was a swing to Paice's playing more characteristic of jazz than rock.

Paice's first foray into rock 'n' roll came with a collective that gloried in the name Georgie and the Rave-Ons, who gigged diligently, but unambitiously, around Oxfordshire. Changing their name to The Shindigs in 1965, Paice began to get distinctly itchy feet, yearning to belong to a much more professional and purposeful outfit[11].

As these diverse talents followed their individual paths, it must be admitted that, in terms of their musical influences, there was little to suggest that *In Rock* lay in their future. Rock 'n' rollers with jazz in the background, it is true that some of this early experience can be heard in tracks such as 'Speed King', but the full-on aural assault for which they would later be responsible is difficult to completely reconcile with the pictures of the clean-cut, clean-shaven young men that they were when all of this was happening.

Enter Ian Gillan.

Of course, Gillan was, relatively speaking, a Johnny-come-lately on the Deep Purple scene, but he got his start in music at around the same time as Blackmore, Lord and Paice. A council house lad from Middlesex, he embodied the no-nonsense working class aesthetic of much heavy rock. As with Ian Paice and Jon Lord, there was music in Gillan's family, but his motivation to go into the business came from wider sources: 'My grandfather, my uncle, was a jazz pianist and there was lots of music in the house. I think it gave me the background, but it didn't inspire me to work as a musician in those days. That didn't happen until I heard the young Elvis, Little Richard, Buddy Holly, back when I was a teenager. The world was changing'[12]. His taste for all things rock 'n' roll is reflected in his early work with such church hall bands as Garth Rockett and the Moonshiners and The Javelins[13]. The Elvis stylings are still evident in the songs that Deep Purple played alongside Lord's 'Concerto' in 1969 and which can be heard on the extended version of that album released as an anniversary disc some years ago. A cover of Jerry Lee Lewis' 'It'll Be Me' can be found on Deep Purple's 2013 release *Now What!?*.

While a member of the Javelins — basically a covers band — Gillan took, for some reason, to calling himself Jess Thunder[14]. Even so, this period represented the first time that he would be paid for performing; it coincided with the moment that the first fuzzbox-based sounds were emerging from America.

Of the final part of the *In Rock* personnel roster, Roger Glover, one thing that can be said about him is that he was — and still is — Welsh. While, for many, that would be biography enough, for Glover, a little more detail is called for. Acquiring his first acoustic guitar in 1959, he has claimed that music 'really took over [his] life,' but, he said, 'only as a fan — I never thought that I would ever be a musician: that seemed too far down the road, until I got my first guitar and that confirmed that I would never be a musician because it was just too difficult'[15].

It was hearing 'Apache' by The Shadows that changed his mind. A seminal instrumental, 'Apache' seems to have been composed for the sole purpose of making young men fall in love with the electric guitar. Thus inspired, Glover went on to form The Madisons, a well-behaved combo of bow tie-wearing young gentlemen who played cover versions of the day's popular songs at local events. In that increasingly fulcrum-like year of 1962, the band joined forces with another group called The Lightnings, who would go on to become Episode Six — a far more significant part of this story[16].

Meanwhile, Blackmore was making progress, albeit of

a stuttering kind. He joined The Outlaws, a kind of house backing band for the producer Joe Meek, whose clients included Tom Jones and Heinz Burt[17]. Blackmore would continue to be a part of the latter's permanent backing band [briefly The Wild Ones before changing to The Wild Boys], even after The Outlaws gave up the gig.

Videos of Heinz and his band's performances suggest that they were something of an anachronism, even for the early '60s. Sporting DAs and Teddy Boy-style lounge suits, they look like they are playing at a wedding from sometime in the mid-1950s. Given the musical revolutions already in train across the Atlantic, it all has a rather quaint air that has not aged well. That said, Burt's song, 'Just Like Eddie' does include some plucked guitar — by Blackmore — that stands out from the rest of the music. Not far away from a rock riff, it is easily the most interesting feature of an otherwise bland tune.

On the plus side, this period was good for Blackmore's image, as he told *Rolling Stone* magazine: 'All the big groups knew and raved about me. We played with the Stones once and Mick Jagger said in an interview that I was the best guitarist he'd ever seen. The next I slagged the Stones in print and that was the end of that friendship. Still, I was well respected, from top to bottom'[18].

The slight edge of arrogance here, combined with the tendency towards dissatisfaction that would largely result in the 'mark' system for Deep Purple line-ups (not to mention a bewildering array of hirings and firings in his solo project Rainbow), led Blackmore to feel constrained by his association with Burt. So, he joined an outfit called The Crusaders, before re-teaming with Sutch.

A period of pinballing between these two jobs — broken by a brief residency in Italy — came to an end when, realising that much of his live work was happening in Germany, he moved there on a semi-permanent basis, renting a flat in Hamburg. He rationalised this by arguing that the scene in Britain was simply not ready for what he could offer: 'Everywhere you looked, all you could see were these pretty faces — the Hollies, the Beatles.... I moved to Hamburg, Germany, for a few years. Meanwhile, I practised five hours a day. Finally, Hendrix hit it big in England. I figured it was safe again, so I moved back'[19].

Lord joined The Artwoods (named for their leader, Art Wood, older brother of The Rolling Stones' Ronnie Wood). Gaining a record deal, the band put out a number of singles, but made few inroads into the market, achieving only modest chart success. Still, in terms of *In Rock* DNA, they are arguably more important than anything that Blackmore was doing at the time. The Artwoods song 'Keep Lookin'', for example, sounds archaic today, but it starts with an organ solo that is not unlike the one to be found at the top of 'Speed King'. Another similarity is the drum beat followed immediately by the first verse. The chugging riff also anticipates many of those that would come to characterise Deep Purple's brand of hard rock.

Lord also did a session with The Kinks in 1964. Although Lord himself frequently said he provided the piano parts for The Kinks' proto-fuzzbox classic, 'You Really Got Me', the piano on the released version was actually played by Art Greenslade. There was an earlier, unreleased version that Lord might have played on but he did play organ on 'Bald Headed Woman', which also appeared on The Kinks' eponymous debut album.

Paice was head-hunted by a band called The Horizons, whose ambition appealed to him. They soon changed their name to MI5 and then The Maze, under both of which, they achieved some success. MI5's single, 'You'll Never Stop Me Loving You' is a typical piece of '60s crooned easy listening music, but that is not important for this story — what is, was the identity of the crooner, a certain Rod

Evans. Evans' voice was very much of its time, deep and manly, but prone to sentimentality — all of which was fine for the bands in which he was playing.

The Horizons toured extensively, going beyond their home shores and even scoring gigs, like Blackmore, in Hamburg. The Maze went on to play that strangely significant German city, too, and, on one such trip, Paice and Evans first encountered Blackmore. Paice explained that he met the guitarist on a ferry travelling from Dover to Ostend; he takes up the story: 'We all knew who [Blackmore] was. He was already a name amongst British musicians. We knew of the great guitarist. But I just saw him — I didn't actually meet him. He was on his way back home to Hamburg'[20]. He goes on, 'We went up to Hamburg, to play the Star Club, which was a different world to now... Hard work. It was hard, but when you're kids, you can do anything and we were kids... Ritchie was in the audience one night and he came up and said hello and said how much he enjoyed my playing. So that was a really nice thing. I felt really good about it, but we finished the shows and we went back to the UK and I thought nothing more about it'[21].

The Maze as a band have weathered somewhat better than many of the others considered here. While not much of a match for the bombast of *In Rock*, a track like 'Non Fatemi Odiari' looks forward to the material of what would come to be known as Deep Purple Mark I — to which two of its creators would contribute. Melodic, romantic, at times melodramatic, it suits Rod Evans' voice very well, although it is a little too subdued to be a major showcase for Paice's talents.

As the '60s wore on towards their inevitable climax, the chess pieces that were the future members of Deep Purple - now anywhere between five and seven years into their fledgling careers — were arranging themselves

more and more serendipitously on the board. The Mark
I singer Rod Evans was happily ensconced in The Maze
with Ian Paice and, by chance, another founding member,
Nick Simper, found a job in a band with Jon Lord.

Simper was at a loose end after the Pirates had failed
to keep going in the wake of Johnny Kidd's death. As it
happens, he, too, had run into Blackmore while touring
in Germany: 'We bumped into Ritchie and he was doing
nothing at all... he was getting a reputation, just by
walking up to the Star Club and sitting in with people and
jamming'[22].

As for Lord, The Artwoods, following an ill-advised
name change (to the evocative, but not easily said, 'The
St Valentine's Day Massacre') had folded, leaving him to
make ends meet with session work. Winding up in The
Garden, the backing band for The Flower Pot Men, proved
to be particularly fortuitous; as he put it himself: 'I went on
tour with them and at about that time I was getting into
some of the things I'd heard from West Coast groups'[23].
Simper had also been conscripted into the band and
conversations between him and Lord pointed to future
directions, not least in Simper's enthusiasm to work with
a certain Hamburg-based guitarist.

Listening to The Flower Pot Men now is an unusual
experience. Boasting several singers, they were basically
a harmony group with backing, but the two parts make
for a far from seamless match. On their hit single, 'Let's
Go To San Francisco', the music has more than a hint of
psychedelia about it, but it is juxtaposed against high-
pitched singing of the type often to be found on Radio
Two on a Sunday afternoon. The song is certainly dated,
but not in the good way that The Rolling Stones' first few
albums are.

Over in Episode Six, original vocalist Andy Ross, tiring
of residencies in which lengthy sets were punctuated by

the smallest of breaks, decided to get married and leave the music industry forever. Gloria Bristow — or 'Glorious Bristols', as she became known — who worked for the band's management company, went to check out a possible replacement on the recommendation of a colleague. The person in question was slumming it as the lead singer with a group calling itself Wainwright's Gentlemen; he turned out to be one Ian Gillan[24]. Attracted more by Episode Six's professional status than their carefully curated image, Gillan signed up. The deal was superficially attractive — at least, in parts: thirty-thousand pounds a year for the band (when that was a lot of money) and three quarters of one percent of the royalties, rising to three quarters of three percent after twenty-five years (the hope that the music would still be available that much further on in history being presumptuous, to say the least).

The line-up change happened at much the same time that the band inked a recording contract with Pye[25]. Very singles-orientated, their emphasis was on cover versions, the first effort being a remake of 'Put Yourself in My Shoes', which had originally been recorded by The Hollies. Of far more interest, though, was the B-side, a song called 'That's All I Want', written by Roger Glover. Lyrically, it is about as trite as it gets, but the song is not held back by this and bounces along in a fun way that is not so very different from the kind of direct, driving sound that would eventually fill the two sides of *In Rock*.

A pattern emerged with Episode Six's singles: cover song on the A-side — often at the insistence of the record company — original on the reverse, mostly written by Glover. None made any significant dent on the British charts, but the indifference of the band's home audience was not to be found everywhere. Bizarrely, the band achieved considerable success in, of all places, Beirut, where impressive sales from two record shops briefly made them flavour of the month. It was not enough to keep the momentum going for long, but, as the band released an increasingly desperate collection of Beatles and even Charles Aznavour covers, Glover was quietly refining his songwriting skills, becoming more adept at the craft.

Eventually, his, 'I Can See Through You', was released as an A-side. Sounding today suspiciously like mid-career Spinal Tap, the song is not especially memorable, but it does showcase one easily overlooked aspect of Glover's work — that it is enjoyable. As much as musicians like to talk about their art, they are, when all is said and done, entertainers. A songwriter that can deliver an entertaining track is always going to be highly valued and, despite its ho-hum lyrics and straightforward accompaniment, 'I Can See Through You' does entertain.

Again, however, the result was a commercial disappointment. Disillusioned with Pye, the band signed a new deal with an American label that promised to deliver the long-hoped-for pot of gold. The change coincided with yet more personnel shake-ups. This time a new drummer was recruited in the form of Mick Underwood - a man who merits further discussion.

When mentioning Underwood, we should pause for a moment to remember the whole multitude of musicians who fade in and out of the Deep Purple story, populating the fringes, but without ever quite getting into the centre of the action. Many will recognise Underwood's name from the second time he worked with Gillan in Gillan's Purple hiatus band simply called — er — Gillan, but he was much more central than even that would suggest, crossing paths with the Purple people on numerous occasions.

Accounting for this, he gives a very practical reason, 'Looking back on it now — at the time when I was first getting into playing — Ritchie Blackmore lived about a mile and a half from where I lived. Ian Gillan — who I really didn't know until Episode Six times — lived about two miles away, on the council estate. I met Ritchie when I first got behind a drum kit'[26]. Taught the drums by Jim Marshall — yes, *that* Jim Marshall — he rode on the usual merry-go-round of bands before becoming a part of none other than The Outlaws, playing alongside Blackmore. After Episode Six, he co-founded Quatermass, whose 'Black Sheep of the Family' would be covered twice over by Rainbow. It would also play a significant role in the ultimate fate of Deep Purple.

Of his musical network, Underwood has said: 'When you look back on it, you say, 'God, these are the top echelon'. They're great players and they're great to work with. As a musician, when you play with great guys, it rubs off on you... and you play better'[27]. To Underwood's name could be added those of, for example, Tony Ashton, Cozy Powell, perhaps Bernie Marsden: all great in their own right, but destined to orbit the gas giant that is Deep Purple from afar. Underwood would, however, go on to play a role in the making of *In Rock* which, small at the time, can be seen as enormous with the benefit of some of that good old hindsight.

The new Episode Six line-up continued to put in the hours, but it was just not happening for them in any major way. Another label change made very little difference. The most notable output at this stage was the B-side of the single, 'Lucky Sunday', a song called 'Mr Universe', from which, in something of a rerun of the 'Black Night' writing process, the band Gillan would later steal the title[28].

The year 1967 was significant for a number of reasons — not the least of which being that it was when your humble author was born. More relevantly for this story, it was the point at which the different future members of Deep Purple began to coalesce, not that they had any idea of that at the time. Gillan and Glover were working together, as were Simper and Lord and so were Evans and Paice. Over the water, the prince, Blackmore, was biding his time, waiting for something to happen that would justify a return.

Again, it would be all too easy to see what happened next as inevitable, but that cannot have been how it seemed to the people involved. For a start, they were all producing the type of light poppy fare that most characterised the age and had little to do with anything that they would go on to produce. There were hints of what was to come, but they were relatively few and are only really revealed as hints by yet more hindsight. Career-wise, everyone was doing quite well, without getting anywhere near the big time. Blackmore may have had a bigger following than most, but it was not translating into money in the bank. He must have seriously wondered when all the effort and hard work were going to pay off. A catalyst was needed to cause the necessary series of actions and reactions that would bring all of the scattered talents together.

That catalyst was not an object, or an event. It was a man. A man who went under the deceptively ordinary name of Chris Curtis (although that was a pseudonym, his actual name being the decidedly more interesting — if a gift to his critics — Chris Crummey). His importance to the formation of what would become Deep Purple was acknowledged by Blackmore: 'He did get everyone together. It was his band. For what it was worth. A very important person: without Chris Curtis, it would not have happened'[29].

Born in the not conspicuously rock 'n' roll town of Oldham in Lancashire, Curtis went to school in Liverpool before joining the already established skiffle-based band The Searchers in 1962 as drummer. The Searchers were about to hit the crest of a wave, having spent time building their act at the Star Club in Hamburg (it must be admitted that — for all of my talk of hindsight — there are some moments of serendipity in this story). With The Beatles dominating popular music, The Searchers did not have to do much more than be Liverpudlian to get their first recording contract with Pye[30]; as Curtis said: 'The Beatles had just hit and Les Ackerley, the manager of the Iron Door club, told us to put some songs on tape. He let us have the club for an afternoon and we got a weeny tape recorder and recorded the whole act. He took it to Decca who didn't want it, but then he took it to Pye. Tony Hatch jumped at it as he wanted to be George Martin to The Searchers or at least, he wanted to be on the bandwagon. 'Sweets For My Sweet' was on the tape and he asked us to record that for our first session'[31].

'Sweets For My Sweet' went on to be a number one hit. It was only the first of several big sellers, including 'Needles and Pins', of which Curtis said: 'If you haven't got the listeners in the first few seconds, you haven't got them, and we had them with that. That opening A chord on 'Needles and Pins' will never be topped. It must have been a good riff as The Byrds have used it countless times — upside down, this way, that way'[32]. Obviously, these were all achievements which the others that we have considered could only have dreamed of at this point.

Curtis' run in The Searchers was every bit as tempestuous as it was successful. Acrimonious line-up changes, arguments, tantrums and plenty of pharmaceuticals were the leitmotifs. Matters came to a head in Australia, where The Searchers were placed on a bill with The Rolling Stones, against whom they came off decisively second best. After a night at the home of a star-struck young female groupie, Curtis injured his finger in a door, putting in doubt his continued participation in the tour. He opted for a more permanent divorce and quit the band altogether[33].

Newly emancipated, Curtis did some producing for the likes of Paul and Barry Ryan and put out a single with Alma Cogan. His major solo effort, a single called 'Aggravation', is most notable for its backing band, which was loaded with future rock stars, including Jimmy Page and John Paul Jones. It is fanciful to suppose that this might have been the seed of another idea that Curtis was mulling over — to put together a band that would be harder and heavier than the light, jaunty groups that were filling the airwaves all around him. He just needed to find the right people...

So a watershed moment was reached, although, again, that can only be said in retrospect. What was undoubtedly true was that the personnel were all ready, hungry for something more and increasingly open to making themselves available. All they needed was for Chris Curtis to reach out and invite them in.

As for Tommy Steele: he had recently starred in the film musical *Half A Sixpence*.

Sculpting In Rock

4
REHEARSALS

Tony Edwards was the kind of character who appears in fat, multi-generational novels concerned with business and family, all played out against an ever-changing historical backdrop. He was the kind of character who was probably once common in London, but who would seem a little out of place now. Born in the early 1930s, he spent much of his life in the rag trade, working principally for his mother. His was not though, a (again, pardon the pun) rags-to-riches tale. Thanks to rags, he was rich from the get-go, a graduate of the LSE who spent much of the early '60s cruising around London in a Jensen sports car.

By the middle of the decade, he had begun to tire of that life. His dreams were taking him towards showbiz — in particular, the popular music end of showbiz. Again, from a modern perspective, it seems obvious that there was money to be made in that area: the Brian Epsteins, Colonel Tom Parkers, Joe Meekses and many others more than prove the point. But, it is easy to forget that the pop music industry was relatively new at the time. Rock 'n' roll had emerged only a few years earlier in the US and Tommy Steele's successes were still in the recent past. The world of popular music must have seemed as much of a new financial frontier as home computers and smartphones would decades later.

Fired up by not much more than self-belief and blind enthusiasm, Edwards began by attempting to influence the career of model-turned singer Ayshea (Brough). A purveyor of highly melodic, but ultimately disposable, pop songs, Ayshea has not lingered long in the collective memory, but she was a good enough bet for Edwards to befriend Vicki Wickham, the producer of musical TV show *Ready Steady Go*, on her behalf[1].

Thanks to Wickham, Edwards met Chris Curtis and listened to his ideas for a new band. Although some were a little off-the-wall, to put it mildly, Edwards found himself getting increasingly drawn in. Envisioning something called Roundabout, Curtis argued that the name would also be the enterprise's chief organising principle. In his mind, it would apply to a band consisting of three core musicians who would be permanent members, while others would be recruited as and when their talents were required. They would, in a very real sense, board the roundabout for a quick ride, only to make way for new punters when the Wurlitzer music and the spinning stopped[2]. Somewhat inexperienced and, at this stage, perhaps a little naïve, Edwards agreed to bankroll this wackiness, despite his own misgivings: 'I financed the concept', he said, 'All my personal shareholdings in the family business were there as collateral for financing equipment, subsistence, rents. I don't think I was familiar with the sort of music they were creating. I was rather aghast, but I believed in artistic integrity and felt they knew better than I did'[3].

Realising that he might be in over his head, Edwards recruited two other key figures on to the management team. One, Ron Hire, was primarily a money man, who served to ease some of Edward's financial burden. In a typical piece of 'only back then'ness, Hire had begun as a used car salesman. The other newcomer was both more hands-on and a more obvious pick for the role. John Coletta would go on to later manage Whitesnake, but, prior to his involvement with Edwards, he had been a partner in an advertising and marketing consultancy[4]. Forces joined, the three businessmen quickly came up with HEC Enterprises, a name based on their last initials[5].

At the creative end, the main question was who would be the three at the heart of things? On drums, of course, would be Curtis. Keyboards would be played by someone who Curtis found 'living in a dump'[6]: Jon Lord. The other was a guitarist who he claimed to have had flown in to England especially for the occasion, Ritchie Blackmore, although there is some doubt as to whether Blackmore showed up at all at the start. He claimed that: 'When [Curtis] wanted to put a band together, he sent me all these telegrams in Hamburg and called me over. I came over and it was — all very Monty Python — he was very animated and very theatrical'[7]. In any case, neither Lord nor Blackmore seemed very enthusiastic about what was on offer. Lord's major worry was job security: 'It was going to be called Roundabout, because roundabouts, man, go round and round and you get on and off a roundabout, don't you, you know what I mean, man? I said, 'yes'. So anybody can be in the band because those that want to be will get on the roundabout and stay on as long as they want and then they'll get off the roundabout. Yes, I said, does this mean that I can be pushed off the roundabout? He said, 'No, you and I, Jon, will be the core'[8].

Blackmore's experience was equally bizarre: 'I asked [Curtis], who's in the band, what's the deal? And he would go, 'The best guitarist in the world is you... you're in the band, you'll be playing second guitar'. So you'll [Curtis] be playing lead, right? Who will be playing drums? 'I'll [Curtis] be playing drums'. Jon Lord? 'Jon Lord will be playing organ'. It was going to be called The Light. And then he said, 'and I will be playing bass and vocals'! So, he was playing lead guitar, drums, bass and vocals! So when I saw Jon, I said, 'What's going on?'"[9].

Curtis moved into Lord's 'dump' and promptly covered everything with silver paper in order to 'keep the vibes in'. Vacating the place after a few months (owing his half of the rent), he left his erstwhile roomy none the wiser as to where Roundabout might actually be going (apart from round and round in metaphorical circles).

The drummer's increasingly bizarre behaviour led to him being unceremoniously dropped. His own take is that Edwards was behind the move: 'He thought I wasn't right for the group and they left me behind... He arranged for them to record a song that I had been playing to Jon Lord for months, 'Hush'"[10]. This last claim will be revisited, but the other parts, too, are open to dispute.

According to Edwards, contact with Curtis was simply lost[11]. Other versions have it that Blackmore and Lord were the ones who walked away, the former heading back to Germany. Lord then began to talk to HEC about a new — different — band that would have a more conventional composition[12]. Quite how long Curtis continued to hang around is uncertain; Nick Simper has suggested that he was still hovering in the background even after the new band had found its first line-up and set about recording a demo[13].

The truth is no doubt an average of the contents of a lot of old men's memories, but what can be stated with confidence is that Curtis, having got the project — sort of — off the ground, left it, probably forever, some time in late 1967. Strangely, his future lay in a tax office, in which he worked as a clerk, presumably contentedly, for the better part of two decades.

A seed had been planted, but the chances of it growing

from its stony ground and flowering into anything especially noteworthy had gone from 'slim' to 'next-to-non-existent'. It seems that only the tenacity of a combined Edwards and Lord kept the project alive. Blackmore was persuaded to give it another try and was brought back over from Germany, paying Lord an unexpected visit. Lord said of the momentous get-together: 'Ritchie came to the flat, which I de-foiled. He appeared at my door in a snowstorm, carrying an acoustic guitar. That night we came up with two of the songs that went on the first [Deep Purple] album, 'And the Address' and 'Mandrake Root'. It was a wonderful evening. Right away I felt that he wouldn't suffer fools gladly, but it felt right. Ritchie seemed dark; he always seemed dark'[(14)]. The two clearly got on well enough, but Blackmore refused to commit, making the — frankly, far from unreasonable — demand that he would need to see which other musicians were involved.

A press report published in the *New Musical Express* on 6th January 1968 claimed, 'Curtis has formed a new group of five multi-instrumentalists, which he will record individually and as a team. Named Roundabout, the group is rehearsing all this month, and at the end of January will cut its first LP, 'Get On'. Curtis is also planning a specially produced stage show complete with visual effects — the show will be a complete package, incorporating its own supporting acts and including another group formed by Curtis called Gates of Heaven. Personnel of the Roundabout comprises John Lord, Robbie Hewlett, Kenny Mudie, Ritchie Blackmore, Chris Curtis and another musician who cannot be named'.

Whatever the accuracy or not of that report, Curtis was soon out of the picture for good. A direct replacement for Curtis was found in the form of the well-respected drummer Bobby Woodman. He had been on the scene since the late 50s, playing with such artists as Vince Taylor and a very youthful Jimmy Page. It would not be too much to say that he was quite a catch for the band. He had been working in Paris with a bass player called Dave Curtiss, who came along for the ride. Curtiss, however, was less convinced that the nascent band had any real idea of what it wanted to achieve and swiftly departed. A more permanent bassist was suggested by Lord: Nick Simper, his Flowerpot Men colleague.

The attraction for Simper was not, as it happens, the core group, but Woodman: 'I didn't take a lot of interest until I heard Bobby Woodman was on drums,' he said, 'I was a little bit in awe of Bobby because of his pedigree and desperately wanted to be in a band with him. Jon said 'I'm getting this new thing together, would you give this up for twenty-five pounds a week?' We were earning mega money with The Flowerpot Men but, because of Bobby Woodman, I said 'yeah, just watch me'[15].

Again, the chronology is open to question, as Simper has stated that he was already in the band when Chris Curtis returned: 'Actually, he turned up later at the studios with that orange label demo. He walked in and we said, 'what are you doing here?' and he said 'Tony Edwards asked me down'. He said, 'I'm going to produce this' and Ritchie said, 'well, if you're going to fucking produce it, I'm not going to play on it' and walked out'[16].

Be that as it may, something like a band was beginning to take shape: Blackmore on guitar, Lord on keyboards, Simper on bass and Woodman on drums. All that was needed was a vocalist. Ensconced, at HEC's expense, in Deeves Hall, a farmhouse in South Mimms, Hertfordshire[17], the nearly-band set about rehearsing and recruiting. The first pick was Terry Reid, but he turned the job down (he would subsequently do likewise when offered the front man role with a group provisionally named The New Yardbirds...), possibly under pressure from his manager, that other larger-than-life personality, Mickie Most.

Simper proposed offering the job to a vocalist he had seen live a number of times: 'One night, we had a party — invited a few friends — and Tony Tacon came along. I said, 'we needed a singer' and he said, 'what about Gillan?' And I said, 'yeah, what's he doing?' He was with Episode Six... and I said to Tony, 'would you ask him, tell him what we've got, cos you've seen it all' — he was obviously impressed — banks of Marshalls, nice big house! 'Tell Gillan what it's all about — ask him if he's interested in coming down'[18].

Gillan was not. He believed that Episode Six were on the verge of a breakthrough and could see no reason to leave them in order to jump on Roundabout's merry-go-round — especially as it seemed to consist of not much more than a few businessmen with more money than sense and a load of directionless musicians-for-hire.

With desperation setting in, an advert was placed in *Melody Maker*, the wording of which was bullish, to say the least: 'An incredible vocalist required for incredible newly-formed group. Two months well-paid rehearsal in own country mansion. We are professionals, if you are not, please don't apply. Equipment supplied. Success guaranteed.' A vocalist they may have lacked; self-belief was not so much of a problem.

A mob of the hopeful and the hopeless descended upon Deeves Hall to try their luck. All were swiftly shown the door, except one, Mick Angus, who went away confident that the gig was his. It so happened that he was a long-standing friend of the lead singer with The Maze, Rod Evans, to whom he naturally spoke of his success. Intrigued, Evans took the trip down to Deeves Hall himself and promptly got the job over Angus. His vocals were his chief selling point, but his idea to cover The Beatles'

'Help!' as a ballad also impressed the other members of a band still grappling to find an identity. Woodman was not particularly sold on the new recruit, criticising his voice for sounding too much like that of Frank Sinatra.

This was only one of many ways in which Woodman was beginning to appear out of his element. Musically, too, he was not fitting in, having little interest in the direction in which the others were going. Another service that Evans did for his new colleagues was to suggest a replacement: the drummer he had until very recently been working with in The Maze. Ian Paice takes up the story: 'In early 1968, Rod Evans — wonderful guy — felt that our band was actually going nowhere; he was probably right and he saw an advert in the *Melody Maker* magazine for a new band that required a singer. So he applied for the job and when he got there, he found it was Ritchie Blackmore, Jon Lord, Nicky Simper. Ritchie recognised Rod from the year before: he said, 'have you still got the drummer?' Rod said yeah. Ritchie said, 'you've got to bring him along'. So that's what happened. So the first time I met Ritchie was outside a train station... Anyway, he arrived in Nick Simper's Jaguar and they drove me back to the hall, Deeves Hall, where the band were set up to practise. They already had a drummer in place, a really good, experienced, drummer. His name was Bobby Woodman. I got the impression it wasn't really working between Bobby and Ritchie and Jon and Nick. His kit was set up there: now that's a problem. As far as I remember it, Bobby was asked, or coerced, to nip down to the village to get some cigarettes, or something like that. That was a ploy to get him out of the house — which he duly did. While he was away, I sat down on his drum kit and I stole his gig. There's not much you can say about it, other than that. Looking back, when you get a chance to move up in the music industry, you have to take it'[19].

A line-up now in place, priority number one was to record something, so a two track demo was made as a calling card to record companies.

On one side was a song called 'Shadows'. Credited to the whole band, it was locked in a vault until it was rather apologetically put out on the *Anthology* compilation album in 1985 — an ignominious fate for what is a very interesting track. It must firstly be admitted that it is very catchy: the chorus, despite being sung in typical '60s falsetto style, is a great hook that sticks in the mind. The main riff, too, has something of the *In Rocks* about it, although fuzzbox distortion is not much in evidence.

In fact, the solo is played using a wah-wah pedal. This effect — much loved by disco artists of the '70s — was another way to distort a guitar sound, this time so that it resembled the human voice, especially a human voice speaking the syllable 'wah'[20]. It was to become the signature sound of the first iteration of Deep Purple, its rather tortuous meanderings gracing a good percentage of any given album. As we have seen, it can be heard briefly on *In Rock*, but, afterwards, it was largely rejected in favour of the fuzzbox. It is difficult to think of any wah-wah-infused songs on subsequent albums.

The other demo song was an instrumental version of the band composition 'Love Help Me', a sung version of which would be recorded later. By all accounts, the demo version was not intended to be an instrumental; it ended up as one because of a mistake by an engineer. In many ways, this was a felicitous accident, because what is revealed by the removal of the rather tedious vocals is proto-hard rock at its best. Yes, it is another wah-wah fest, but that aside, the track has a tough-as-old-boots riff, a pounding bass line and more than a hint of fuzz. It is easy to see where this type of creativity might lead, but where it came from is less obvious: is the guitar line by the same guy who was strumming on 'Just Like Eddie' a few short years earlier?

It perhaps had something to do with the band's acknowledged influence at this stage, American psychedelics Vanilla Fudge. Simper has explained that, 'I was so amazed when I saw Vanilla Fudge,' going on, 'The whole style of what they were doing, the way they were playing sort of — how can you describe it? Like panache. You know the way they set about it. Everyone just came out and watched these guys'[21]. Simper also made the good point that music was changing. Where he and his contemporaries had been in pop groups hitherto, now they were part of bands; as he put it, everyone knew that music was changing, but no-one was quite sure what it was changing into.

The members of Roundabout, as it was still called, were in a good position to catch the crest of that wave, but were still relatively inexperienced as songwriters. Blackmore, for all the creativity he would go on to show, had spent most of his career in backing bands — he had not been called upon to do much more than play. Likewise, Lord had few original compositions to his credit. Under the circumstances, Vanilla Fudge — in the vanguard and with a recognisable style — must have seemed like a good example to follow.

It was not just the sound that appealed. Blackmore and Co. — especially Simper — were also aware that the band needed a look, an image. Much time was spent developing one. Hair — which burst through the slicked back styles to become long and unkempt — and clothes — Blackmore began to put together his characteristic 'man in black' look: black everything, boots and a pilgrim-style hat — were only part of the package. Moves were also important. The guitar-wielders began to throw shapes on stage, broadening their stance, throwing their instruments around, striding restlessly about. It would all bear fruit in the long run, when such antics would find their natural home as part of arena-scale shows, but they caused considerable bemusement among the audiences of the band's earliest English shows, most of which took place at smallish venues and clubs.

The '60s may have been a time of massive social change, but provincial England was not exactly ahead of the curve: watching long-haired freaky people behaving like idiots was not yet most people's idea of a fun evening out.

Anyway, HEC's second major job (after 'pay for stuff') was 'get a recording contract', which they were not sufficiently well-connected to be able to accomplish. Instead, Blackmore got in touch with his old friend, the producer, Derek Lawrence, who, now working for EMI, had a listen to some Deeves Hall rehearsals and, on the strength of those, got the band their first deal [22].

They were on their way.

Sculpting In Rock

5
SHADES

Thanks to Lawrence's efforts, the band were signed to the EMI label Parlophone in the UK. More significant in the early days, though, was their USA home, which would rapidly become both a blessing and a curse. Largely backed by the money of comedian Bill Cosby, Tetragrammaton approached Lawrence touting for business and gratefully accepted his suggestion that Blackmore and Co. be among their signings[1].

The weeks at Deeves Hall had not been wasted and a body of material, consisting of originals and cover versions, had been assembled. It would go on to form the content of the band's debut album, but, first of all, it needed to be road tested, so the band decided to embark on a short tour of Scandinavia. This odd choice seems to have been motivated by that region's love for The Artwoods, which, it was felt, would translate into curiosity-driven ticket sales among Lord's presumed fan base. An interesting side note is what this implies about power dynamics within the band at this point. Blackmore may have been the musician's musician, but Lord was perceived to be the bigger draw with the public — the Scandinavian public, at any rate.

There was a problem around what name would appear on those as yet unprinted tickets. Even on the ferry over to Scandinavia, no one was certain as to what the band would be called in the long term. Officially still Roundabout, only Edwards was happy with that particular status quo. A wide range of alternatives was mooted. Lord recalled Orpheus being one, along with the distinctly Led Zeppelin/Iron Butterflyish Concrete God. Fire was another possibility, although that sounds more suitable for a soul band. In the end, they did not find their name because it, like all good rock band names, found them. It was put forward by Blackmore, who thought of it because it was the title of his grandmother's favourite song — or, anyway, a song that she liked to play. Initially disregarded, rather than rejected, Blackmore, for want of anything better, came back to it several times, before it was bluntly announced to the press as though it had always been the band's name.

Deep Purple[2].

It is now so familiar that it is easy to forget what a stroke of genius it is. The rather quirky way in which Blackmore came up with it perhaps indicates that he was not expecting this band to last any longer than all of the others with which he had been associated over the years, but that should not disguise the name's impact. 'Deep Purple' stands out: it is not pretentious, or wilfully whimsical, it does not sound like it is imitating the name of any other band — except insofar as putting a colour into the name of a band was fashionable at the time — and it is reasonably non-committal about the style of music to which it is attached.

Over the course of what has proven to be decades, 'Deep Purple' has been a hospitable space for rock, psychedelia, funk, folk, prog, classical — you name it. It is difficult to imagine a band called Black Sabbath producing anything other than hard rock.

There are no reports of dissenters. The name was

accepted by all. The five musicians, assembled with so much difficulty, would go out into the world — or, anyway, Scandinavia — under the name Deep Purple.

Their first ever gig was in a packed school hall in Tastrup, Denmark, on April 20th 1968. The evening got off to an inauspicious start, as the band disembarked from the ferry only to be bundled into waiting police vans; a mix-up over permits meant that they were technically in the country illegally. By the time everything was sorted out, there was little time left to prepare for the gig. But, still it went ahead — the band were, as they had said themselves, professionals.

Simper remembered the occasion as being less about the music — which was laced with many a 'bum note' — than image, with he and Blackmore putting more effort into the stage moves that they had perfected in front of the mirrors of Deeves Hall[3].

The opener was 'And the Address', one of the tunes that Blackmore and Lord had worked on during that evening in Lord's flat. An instrumental, it is a strange choice to programme so early in the proceedings, in that it completely sidelines the vocalist. But, it serves well to build the atmosphere, being a high tempo rocker with more than a hint of heaviness to it.

'Hush', with which the band would go on to have a long and storied history, was also included. Written by Joe South, it is effectively a reworking of a spiritual dating all the way back to 1923. Although Chris Curtis claimed to have brought it to the band, it was, in fact, quite big that year. It had already been recorded in quick succession by several artists, most notably Billy Joe Royal. Blackmore claimed to have heard it in Germany and Simper also spoke about knowing the song before his involvement with Roundabout/Deep Purple[4]. In conversation with me, he stated that the band just started to play it one day during the rehearsal period, liked it, and put together an arrangement there and then.

Other items on the menu were 'Hey Joe', reflecting, more than anything, Blackmore's growing admiration for Hendrix. 'Love Help Me' — presumably with vocals — was given an airing, as was the band's weirdly unentertaining ballad version of The Beatles' 'Help!'.

Best of the night would certainly have been 'Mandrake Root'. Ostensibly an original, it is another song that demonstrates Blackmore's penchant for what could charitably be called quoting from the work of others. The song has an interesting and unusual structure, the first half consisting of a couple of brief verses and choruses, before a long instrumental section kicks in, during which the guitar and keyboards do their thing over a simple throbbing bass and drum backing. Neither part is without musical antecedents. The main riff is a straight lift from a song called 'Lost Soul' by Bill Parkinson, who, like Blackmore, had played for Screaming Lord Sutch in a former life. It is overlaid on a basic track that is not far from a cover version of Hendrix's 'Foxy Lady'. Parkinson made enough of a fuss to earn himself a cash settlement (HEC's pockets must have been deep); it is not known what Hendrix thought about it all. Notwithstanding any of that, 'Mandrake Root' remains a tremendous piece of heavy rock that undoubtedly has the DNA of Deep Purple's later marks written into it: it would remain a live staple for a considerable time to come.

The set was padded out with an extended run-through of Cream's 'I'm So Glad' and another original, the underwhelming 'One More Rainy Day'[5].

While the tour was a success, to the extent of generating some media interest (no mean feat for a new band with no recorded product), it allowed no room for complacency. Returning to England, the band were almost immediately booked into a studio to lay down their first album. Lord remembered this as a less than enjoyable experience: 'We didn't 'go' — we were 'put' into a recording studio and told to make an album. We were given twenty-four hours. It was in those days... so, we did everything we'd been rehearsing. Made an album out of it... The mixing took — well, if you listen back to *Shades of Deep Purple*, which was the album, it took about nine minutes, I think. We weren't allowed to even touch it, you know'[6].

Derek Lawrence produced, but, given the constraints, could only achieve so much. As a consequence, 'Shades' does not have the greatest sound — or, anyway, it didn't until remastered versions were released in the early twenty-first century. Where the album could be enlivened with booms and bangs and growls, it sounds subdued and muddy. 'Mandrake Root', in particular, loses much of its inherent power.

The dizzying speed of recording was echoed in the release pattern — at least in the USA, where Tetragrammaton put the record out in July. Parlophone were somewhat tardier, waiting until September — by which time, it was already in danger of becoming old news.

As a piece of work, *Shades of Deep Purple* has grown in the minds of loyal fans to become more significant than it perhaps should be. That it is still available has more to do with the existence of 'Smoke on the Water' than its own merits. Initial reviews were mixed. In its home country, few were convinced. At the 'good' end of the spectrum was *Record Mirror*, which said of it, 'Try any track — they're all great. Strongly recommended to all discerning pop fans'[7]. Others were less generous, complaining that the band were too American in style, the Vanilla Fudge influence receiving especially short shrift.

In the USA, the response was more positive.

Ian Paice put the disparity down to the type of music that the band was playing: 'We try to incorporate classical music into pop. John [sic] Lord, our organist, was trained as a classical pianist and he joins it all together. We all do the arrangements together and he supplies the classical knowledge. The result puzzles audiences who are expecting Sam and Dave stuff'. He added that, 'As far as we are concerned, dancing audiences are out. There are only about three numbers in our act that they can dance to'[8].

In truth, 'Shades' is an only sporadically enjoyable confection. Psychedelic and proggy, it certainly points towards the band's future, but is still rather backward-looking in many respects. Quite apart from the fact that, with four cover versions and four originals, it only vaguely hints at the songwriting potential of the band, it does not sufficiently break with what they had all been doing before coming together. Much of the album sounds not unlike what Blackmore had produced with The Crusaders, with a little Artwoods thrown in for good measure. That is before the Vanilla Fudge element is even considered. Had Deep Purple proven to be a one album wonder, it is not likely that 'Shades' would now be more than the smallest of footnotes in any history of 1960s pop music.

It did yield one major triumph, however. 'Hush' was released as a single and became a huge hit in the USA. *New Musical Express* was sufficiently impressed by such a success from a group of 'unknowns' as to feature it as a news story, noting that: 'Deep Purple, a British group still looking for its first chart success in its own country, is well on its way to winning a Gold Disc in America. Its 'Hush' single — released in the States on the new Tetragrammaton label — has already sold over 600,000 copies during its first four weeks of release and is currently placed at number thirteen in the Billboard Hot 100"[9]. The piece ends by informing readers that tour dates in the USA are imminent.

Jon Lord saw this big moment in his career as a matter of luck (again, his account does not accord exactly with what others have said). As he put it: 'We started to record an album, and then a couple of people from Tetragrammaton records in America came over and heard the record. They said they wanted to release it in the States, and wanted to release 'Hush' as a single. They gave us a big build-up in America — but none of us expected this sort of success"[10].

Unfortunately — as would prove to be the case so often with Deep Purple — this great moment contained within it the seeds of future disaster. 'Hush' was riding high, but the earnings for its composition were going to Joe South. The B-side, though, was taken up with 'One More Rainy Day', a not especially impressive song, but the brainchild of Lord and Evans, who duly pocketed considerable sums in writers' royalties. This particularly annoyed Blackmore, who felt that his contribution was being undervalued. He possibly had a point: in interview after interview, his colleagues, and former colleagues, remark on his massive creative input into any project of which he is a part and yet, here he was watching other people get rich, while he had nothing much to show for his efforts[11].

In June, the band recorded some of their material for a couple of BBC sessions. These generally add little to an understanding of the band's thinking — although the absence of 'Mandrake Root' perhaps indicates what they saw as most palatable to the BBC's audience. The version of 'And the Address' is of most interest. Even heavier than the 'Shades' rendition, it underlined the potential of the track to carry the band towards the sound of *In Rock*. Its place in the set list would soon be usurped by a different, better known, instrumental, but, arguably, that was a loss, since this is by far the rockier tune.

Still, there was little time for brooding on such matters, because the need to take the record on the road was pressing. A handful of gigs in the UK were booked. These did not go well. One, at the Lion Hotel in Warrington, did not even reach its end — although this had more to do with Blackmore inadvertently cutting the cables connecting the instruments to their amps than the hostility of the audience (although, by all accounts, the audience was hostile).

The band's roadie, Ian Hansford, had vivid memories of this occasion: 'Basically the Lion was dance music, Northern Soul, so that didn't go down too well. Ritchie was trying to be flash with his guitar and going up and down the frets with cymbals, threw the cymbal on the floor and cut straight through the PA leads'[12].

Another performance, at the Sunbury Jazz and Blues Festival in August (at which the band was on a high quality bill that featured some top artists of the day), was poorly received by both fans and critics — those critics, anyway, who bothered to notice that Deep Purple had even appeared.

It was becoming clear that home audiences were not yet ready for what the band had to offer. The decision was taken to focus on America and a tour was planned for the last three months of the year. But there was a problem. Tetragrammaton were unconvinced that the eight songs already in the bank would be enough for a headlining act and demanded a second album. So it was that, within a couple of months of recording 'Shades', Deep Purple were back in the studio.

This time, there was no mad rush and the album — like *In Rock* after it — was completed during a number of sessions spread out over several weeks; the final recording happened in October, when the band was on the cusp of leaving for the US. Rehearsals took place not in the bucolic splendour of a country house, but, at first, in the Red Lion pub in Acton High Street, London. Situated next to the local police station, the noise that the band were making meant that a move was soon forced upon them. They headed to a place that would gain greater significance in the future — Hanwell Community Centre[13].

The Book of Taliesyn, as the album ended up being called, is an interesting entry in the band's catalogue, being simultaneously a considerable advance on its predecessor and a case of treading water — or, it might be argued, going backwards. Simper has claimed that it was difficult to put together[14], for various reasons, but they boiled down to uncertainty, indeed tacit disagreement, as to what musical direction the band should be taking. Simper described an undeclared Cold War between himself and Blackmore on one side, who favoured a heavier rock approach, and Lord, whose leanings were more towards the classical and prog-orientated. For the moment, the others were prepared to 'indulge' their keyboard player, but, clearly, a crisis was on its way to being reached.

Of the album itself, the title immediately shows that the band's ambitions had grown. *Shades of Deep Purple* is basically a 'hello, here we are' that says nothing about the music and could have been used by a band from any genre. *The Book of Taliesyn*, on the other hand, has an artistic intent behind it: whatever it means — and it would not have meant much to the average buyer on its release — is presumably answered somewhere in the contents.

The album cover, too, is something new. Gone is the naff band photography, to be replaced with a piece of art that can only be described as a masterpiece of mystical kitsch. Drawn by John Vernon Lord (no relation), it is a busy ink drawing, designed to resemble a medieval illustration, filled with activity, mystery and puzzles. A fun fact is that there really is a Book of Taliesin, a 14th century manuscript that collects together the poetry of the eponymous Welsh bard: the hare and fish drawings on the album's cover allude to some of the more bizarre aspects of his legend, those that include transmutations of people into animals. One of the band's best ever cover designs, it is, in and of itself, a statement of growing confidence.

The same cannot be said unequivocally of the contents of the album. In terms of overall structure, the roadmap laid down by 'Shades' was followed, the track listing consisting of a mixture of originals and cover versions. One influential tweak was that it followed a format that would be repeated not only by its immediate successor, but by all Mark II albums, including, and most notably, *In Rock*: seven songs, including an epic-length jam-fest (albeit that 'Taliesyn's entry in the latter category is no 'Child in Time'). The sound is a considerable improvement on that of 'Shades', since, this time, Lawrence had more time to produce and mix the recordings. Gone are the tiresome sound effects that punctuate the songs of 'Shades' as well as that album's rather flat feel. In their place is a more layered and crisp quality that helps to elevate the material, even as it fails to hide its shortcomings.

Speaking of which, the first question mark would be over those cover versions. For 'Shades' the catalogues of artists that were broadly in sympathy with the band's sensibilities — Hendrix, Cream, Joe South — were raided. All right, The Beatles were there, too, but genre-bending versions of their songs were not unknown even in the '60s, so their presence was more than forgivable.

For 'Taliesyn', the sources of cover versions were far more eclectic — and not necessarily in a good way. The Beatles were back (largely, it seems, because Paul McCartney had enjoyed the 'Shades' version of 'Help!'), but they were joined by Neil Diamond ('Kentucky Woman') and

Ike and Tina Turner (the most direct inspiration for 'River Deep, Mountain High', with which the album concluded). Looking at that list, it is not easy to discern what kind of band Deep Purple were trying to be. Rock? Soul? James Bond theme tune music? Perhaps they were just trying to show off by proving that they could cover literally anything and make it their own? If so, it was not a good look.

None of the cover versions are much of a success. 'We Can Work It Out', despite being preceded by a band-generated instrumental entitled 'Exposition', fails to recapture even the limited appeal of 'Help!'. 'River Deep, Mountain High' is a ten-minute clunker that, for some reason, includes lengthy quotations from Richard Strauss' 'Also Sprach Zarathustra' (in fairness, Nietzsche's Zarathustra does spend quite a lot of time hanging around among mountains). 'Kentucky Woman' is the best, although that is a relative term. Loud, bombastic, but quite good fun, it was released as a single, doing quite well in America without replicating the achievements of 'Hush'. In the UK, predictably, it got nowhere.

If Simper[15] is to be believed, members of the band were every bit as unconvinced about the cover versions, the surgery required to make a folky song such as 'Kentucky Woman' sound like rock being quite extensive.

The originals fare little better, being something of a mixed bag. They do not include anything like a 'Mandrake Root', although they do boast at least one minor classic and they definitely evidence growing skill in songwriting. But they do not resolve the central debate at the heart of this brand of Deep Purple.

'Listen, Learn, Read On' gets proceedings off to a fine start. Essentially a song about the Book of Taliesyn, it binds the album together in ways that nothing on 'Shades' ever did. In that Taliesyn and Zarathustra had in common the status of 'legendary mystical wise man', there may be a larger overall purpose to the album than most commentators have spotted. Whatever the truth of that, the song is one that points very specifically and squarely towards *In Rock* — and beyond. Based around a staccato fuzzbox-heavy main riff, the spoken narrative of the verses is a huge advance on anything to be found on 'Shades'.

'Wring That Neck' is the token instrumental. It went on to enjoy a lengthy afterlife beyond the existence of Mark I and it is easy to see why. Catchy, complex and with plenty of space for soloing, it is an excellent track, although jazzier than the more rock-orientated 'And the Address'. Incidentally, the 'neck' in question is that of a guitar and not a person. Notwithstanding that, the song was often billed as 'Hard Road' in an America more sensitive to such things than the UK.

The final two new songs are more problematic. It should be said that both are admirable examples of songwriting. Musically ambitious, structurally daring and lyrically intelligent, they could not be further away from the campy warblings of a 'One More Rainy Day'. But 'Shield' is a light piece of balladry that recalls The Maze more than it looks forward to what Deep Purple would become. Similarly, 'Anthem' is carried by that overly sentimental crooning that was much loved in the '60s, but had no place in the world of hard rock.

More serious was the song's inclusion of a string section. There is nothing wrong with this, of course. Countless are the bands that have made use of classical musicians to add texture to their work. Deep Purple themselves have frequently collaborated to brilliant effect with entire orchestras. But, at such an early stage in the band's career, bringing in string players posed a difficult question: were Deep Purple an arty pop band — as implied by 'Anthem' — or a hard rock combo prepared to explore the outer reaches of imagination — as hinted at by 'Listen, Learn, Read On'? It was to be over a year before a definitive answer was found — and it would not happen without some unpleasant bloodletting.

Regardless of its broader meanings, *The Book of Taliesyn* did not excite much interest among reviewers, or record buyers. John Peel, writing in *Disc and Music Echo*, opined that: 'Each track is well thought and well played but there is no real excitement there. Side one is the weaker side with their American hit, 'Kentucky Woman,' and a poor version of 'We Can Work It Out.' Also on this side is 'Wring That Neck' which they recorded much better for a recent *Top Gear* [BBC Session]. Side two is by far the more interesting side. It opens with 'Shield' which is very good indeed — freer and more relaxed than anything else on the LP. The second track on this side is an over-dramatic 'Anthem.' Perhaps the best thing about the group is their sense of dynamics and their ability to lead into familiar themes with unfamiliar and beautifully constructed instrumentals. This is demonstrated in 'River Deep, Mountain High' which closes this slightly disappointing album'[16].

Not allowing themselves to be discouraged by the negativity, and with new material in the bag, the band set off in October for the USA, where they stayed for the remainder of the year.

With an audience already locked in by the success of 'Hush', they were booked in to some large venues, ostensibly supporting Cream on what was billed as that combo's farewell tour. Two gigs were held at the Forum in Inglewood, California, one of which, on October 18th, was recorded by Tetragrammaton. Left in a vault, discarded, nearly lost and finally rescued by vigilant fans, it was only officially released in 2002, and is more-or-less the only 'live' album — if it can be called that — attributable to this mark of Deep Purple.

Of the set list, there were a few songs that had been around for a while and three from the just-released (in America — it would not appear in the UK until 1969) 'Taliesyn': 'Kentucky Woman', 'River Deep, Mountain High' and — one of only two originals performed all evening — 'Wring That Neck'. The other was, of course, 'Mandrake Root'.

Matters got off to a perfect start with a powerful version of 'Hush', which was not only the song most familiar to the audience, but, with its moody churn of a riff and ample room for soloing, a barnstorming opening to any gig. Most of the songs clocked in longer than their album versions, a sign that the band was incorporating in this recording some of the improvisation that would become a hallmark of their live performances; 'Mandrake Root' already reaches ten minutes or so — it would end up lasting up to, and over, half an hour when played by Mark II.

Listening to the Inglewood gig now, the overriding impression is of just how confident, not to mention competent, the band were live even at this early stage of their career. The recording is not without a few issues: Evans sometimes sounds out of his depth and 'Mandrake Root' is a little discordant in places, but, on the whole, the band are pretty tight. The lead instruments are — it need hardly be said — to the fore, but Simper's bass lines are a solid foundation and Paice's drumming is fantastic — his work on 'Kentucky Woman' is a masterclass in itself. At the front, Evans is charismatic and aware, adeptly making up for any moments when his vocals become swamped by their backing.

Moreover, the recording is key to the archaeology of *In Rock*. The long instrumental section of 'Mandrake Root' is loaded with the kind of extemporised mayhem that the later album would have in spades. It is certainly not much like the lighter corners of 'Shades' — which would include that album's version of 'Mandrake Root'. Less encouragingly, the set list does feature that slowed down remake of 'Help!'.

The Inglewood dates were important for other reasons. Supposedly, they marked the end of Deep Purple's association with Cream, since they were sacked as support act after only three performances: why this happened depends on which source you consult. One reason may have been the story of Jimi Hendrix going backstage to congratulate the band and to cheekily inform Eric Clapton that he had been made to look second best by Blackmore[17]. Such tales may be apocryphal — the more that one researches the history of Deep Purple in the 1960s, the more one realises that everyone who was there remembers things differently — but they serve to build the legend.

To make up for the loss of the Cream support slot, the management hastily booked new dates, which took the band through a good proportion of the United States, before ending with several nights at the Electric Circus in New York City. One of the more bizarre stops was at the Playboy Club in New York on October 23rd, where they performed 'And the Address' and 'Hush' as part of a televised show introduced by the then-not-especially-ancient Hugh Hefner in the role of old-fart-who-doesn't-get-this-type-of-music. This encounter most certainly happened — the footage exists. To call it cringeworthy would be to put it very mildly[18].

The band returned to the UK at the end of 1968 with a crossroads staring them in the face. Reasonably popular in the US — although whether they had already peaked there would only become clear with, yes, hindsight — but totally unknown in their own country and still struggling to find a musical identity, it must have already been obvious to some within the camp that changes were needed. It was by no means the end of Mark I; another album, more tours and some ruthless decision-making lay ahead, but, having been in existence for less than a year, the clock was already ticking on this line-up of the band.

6
UNDERGROUND

What must it have been like to be one of the first people ever to pick up a Deep Purple single or album, thinking, 'I wonder what these new guys are like?' It is a considerable bragging right, which even those of us more advanced in age are too young to claim. Would those original punters have suspected that they were present at the birth of a classic band that would still be releasing new material and performing it live over fifty years later? Or would they have thought of the band as the latest five-minute wonder who would be replaced by the next gang of hopefuls before the opening track of their first, and probably last, album had finished playing?

Today, Deep Purple fans are more likely than not to be a minimum of middle aged, probably male and inclined to see the band through the prism of nostalgia. It has been posited that the phenomenon of adult fanhood — continuing in older age to cling to the passions of one's younger days — is a psychological protection against 'social ageing' (the sense of becoming entrenched in what one is with little opportunity to change), or a safety blanket against anxiety, or an effort to hold on to an aspect of youth[1]. Fan objects thus become part of the self and an extension of it, playing a key role in an individual's construction of the narrative of their life as they grow and alter over time — they are, in effect, the touchstones of a stable identity in a world of personal and social flux[2].

Speaking as an adult Deep Purple fan who took up the cause at a tender age, I would agree with the last of these, seeing fanhood as a way to remain in touch with the person that I once was. For the greying brigade who follow Deep Purple — or any band of their ilk — fanhood is a part of who they are. They will religiously buy every reissue and album of new material because it matters to them; it defines them. Even if they do not listen to it all that much, it needs to be owned.

That would not have been the case in the '60s. Back then, fandom was a relatively new phenomenon, one that was less an expression of personal identity and more a vehicle for social rebellion. Today, pop music tribalism is relatively superficial and precarious: yes, there are rap fans and rock fans and soul fans and devotees of particular singer-songwriters, but few would allow their lives to be defined by their musical tastes. They are not near-cultists in the same way that previous generations of fans often have been. In the '60s, everything from fashions to friendships might be predicated on how a person saw themselves in relation to their favourite acts. Teddy boys were a thing in the '50s; mods and rockers were squaring off against each other only a few years later.

The genesis of fandom as a phenomenon is generally taken to be so-called Beatlemania[3], when young fans of the mop-headed Scousers took to being prompted by their devotion to indulging in behaviour that was often frankly irrational. Screaming during concerts so loudly that the music was inaudible was common — although, as Ian Hanford, pointed out, low quality amps may also have been a factor in this[4]. The film *A Hard Day's Night* gives a flavour of Beatlemania, especially in the ways in which it impinged upon the lives of the beloved stars.

Beatlemania has been interpreted as a function of how good The Beatles were at managing their image. They were roughly the same age as the people to whom they wished to appeal and became aspirational figures to them. They remained down-to-earth (at least, until *Revolver*) and had an air of accessibility — albeit that this was merely an illusion. Thus, the fans were able to fantasise a personal relationship with their idols: they felt that they knew them as people and not just as remote hero-worship figures. Every time such a fan put on a Beatles record, it was speaking to him, or more likely, her, personally and directly — even as the band's members remained ideal forms, what the fans would like to be if opportunity arose. This differed from, say, 'The Tommy Steele Story', which told of how its eponymous hero went from 'us' to 'them'. The Beatles' legend was more subtle — they were 'us' and 'them' at the same time: Schrodinger's Beatle, anyone?

Given this, two other aspects of Beatlemania are worth noting[5]: that it was female-led and working class in orientation. It started in the band's home city of Liverpool, when starry-eyed young women would fight for space close to the stage of the Cavern Club in the hope of catching the attention of one of their idols.

In other words, Beatlemania was — for all of its frivolity — connected to two potent social movements of the age — calls for greater equality among the classes and women's liberation. Of the latter, the shrill female screaming has been theorised as a revolt against sexual repression[6]. That may be so, but, either way, to dismiss fandom as nothing more than vacuous teenage self-indulgence would be a huge mistake.

The scholarly view is that fandom began as a response of the powerless to the constraints within which they were living. Fandom was 'a collective strategy to form interpretive communities that in their subcultural cohesion evaded the meanings preferred by the 'power bloc'"[7]. Since fandom is manifested primarily in positive emotions towards a celebrity, or some other comparable object, it rarely involves a formal organisation, except, perhaps, a relatively benign fan club. But it does find a home in the sensibilities of individuals, giving it a powerful influence on the changing of attitudes[8]. For example, fandom on the Beatlemania model represents the reversal of objectification. Whereas women had previously been the victims of objectification (and continued to be so in the lyrics of pop and rock songs), pop fans, via fandom, became the ones in control: The Beatles were nothing without the gaze of their fans. This was a small, but important, step in the long journey towards female empowerment.

Hence, when Beatlemania quickly spread to America — where it reached its perfect form — it was another strand in the growing foment of calls for some sort of change. Of course, there was already a thriving counter-culture that could trace its roots back to the 1950s and the so-called 'beat' writers, such as Jack Kerouac, whose *On The Road* is the undeclared Bible of the post-war disaffected young man. Beatlemania was merely the latest incarnation, taking its place alongside civil rights marches and, towards the decade's end, the hippy movement — if movement it can be called. It is a matter of record that The Beatles showed their support for civil rights by contractually obliging promoters to desegregate their audiences[9].

Where, then, did this leave fans of Deep Purple and the type of music that they played? Interestingly, research has found that fans of heavy metal are not — contrary to the image given by their music of choice — aggressive and anti-social, but, for the most part, gentle, well-adjusted types[10]. Of course, as reassuring as this is, it can only really be said to apply to fans of the post-*In Rock* band — and possibly not even to them. Mark I may have leaned towards the heavy on occasion, but they were not heavy metal.

It is difficult, in truth, to imagine that a 'Deep Purple fan' — in the Beatlemania sense — existed during the band's first year in business. The diminishing commercial returns that they experienced when releasing their material would suggest that it was bought by the curious, based solely on its qualities as music: if something appealed, it would be bought, but, if it was perceived as 'not good', it would not be, regardless of the people who created it. 'Hush' struck a chord in spectacular fashion, but this proved to be a lucky one-off, which was not to be repeated until major changes had been made to both ban composition and musical style. Later marks were said by some of the more hysterical commentators to have generated 'Purplemania', but that never happened with Mark I.

In accounting for this, it is worth, first of all, pointing to the lack of public name recognition that the band's members enjoyed prior to joining together. For all that it was assembled as though it were a supergroup, Deep Purple's most prominent early figures, by far, were the two who failed to make the final cut, Chris Curtis and Bobby Woodman. Simper may have been a Pirate, but Johnny Kidd was the main man and the project that bore his name soon folded upon his demise. The Artwoods were likewise named after their leader and The Garden were an anonymous backing band, albeit one that was granted unaccompanied slots at gigs. Blackmore's fame was among his peers, the wider public being largely unaware of his gifts. As for The Maze — not long before Paice and Evans left, the band took up an extended residency in

Milan providing musical accompaniment to a play: hardly the action of chart-storming megastars. As 1968 rumbled on, Deep Purple remained a group of unknowns, with a couple of hit singles to suggest that, at best, they might become (in Donald Rumsfeld's strange, but evocative, phrase) known unknowns.

At this stage, they were actually perceived as an 'underground' band. The phrase was used to describe them in a *New Musical Express* article in September 1968[11] and even as late as the *In Rock* era Tony Prince wrote of them: 'One reads in various interviews with underground-type groups about all the weird ideas the group members have'[12].

Jon Lord, speaking to a Canadian TV interviewer in 1969, explored the idea in typically erudite and thoughtful fashion: 'Groups play a certain way and therefore have created, by playing that way, an audience, which you call the underground... It could mean you or me; it could mean the guy over there... It doesn't any more [imply a resistance movement]'[13].

Without intending to, Lord touched on the main theme of Deep Purple as they were then set up: the confusion as to what type of band they were attempting to be. The lack of focus is glaringly obvious on *The Book of Taliesyn* and it was only going to get worse — until *In Rock* settled matters once and for all. On this basis, the question should not be, 'did Deep Purple in 1968 have a large fan base', but 'which version of Deep Purple had a fan base, if either?'

Picking up on one point from the interview, a marked lack of political meaning or social messaging in the output of early Deep Purple may also have given potential followers little to grasp on to. 'Counter-culture' the music was not. 'Child in Time', for all its abstruse qualities, at least sounds like a rallying call — it is angry and urgent, if not that clear about what. Nothing in Mark I's catalogue — on their first two albums, anyway — matches it. 'Shield' begins with a lyric that could be about social issues a la 'Eleanor Rigby', but it quickly becomes a rather conventional love song. That is the case with all of the tracks on 'Shades' and 'Taliesyn': they are ultimately insubstantial and shallow (although, in fairness, it should be acknowledged that Beatlemania was initially sparked by songs that were not exactly Dylanesque in their lyrical complexity).

Lord's denial that the underground had anything to do with resistance was crucial; in effect, he was accepting that Deep Purple did not have a fandom in the usual sense, simply people who liked their music. He says as much as the interview continues: 'I like to play [in Canada] for the simple reason that I can go on stage and play my instrument, which is the organ, and I know that ninety percent of the audience are going to be listening to what I'm playing, not — they're not there to say 'that's one of the Deep Purple, what a groovy guy, you know, look at the clothes he's wearing, I must get his autograph"[13]. Unfortunately, in answer to the question, 'what is underground music', he was only able to say what it was not — and perhaps that was the problem.

While exact numbers are not easy to find, there is every reason to believe that, for the time being, concerts, in America, if not in Britain, continued to be well attended. As Lord identified though, whether this meant that the band was developing a dedicated fan base was debatable. Arguably, only when *In Rock* tapped into the tropes of hard rock/heavy metal did one begin to emerge.

So, to answer the question with which this chapter began, what must it have been like to be a consumer of Deep Purple content at the beginning? The answer is probably that it was nothing special. A putative record buyer may have picked up 'Hush' because it sounded good, but 'Kentucky Woman' wasn't so great and a whole album's worth of this stuff? Maybe. Maybe not. Deep Purple end users could not be expected to view themselves as a homogeneous group when the band itself could not be described as one: the point at which that synergy would start to be achieved lay some months in the future.

7
CHANGES

Deep Purple spent Christmas 1968 at a luxurious hotel in New York toasting what, on the surface, had been a hugely successful year. With a hit single, an album that had also done well, other recorded material that was gaining recognition and healthy concert fees to their credit, everything seemed to be going spectacularly to plan — especially for a band that had only been around for a few months. That it was all happening solely in America was easy to gloss over; America was, after all, the world's largest market, so where was the problem? One place, sadly, was that, the promising start notwithstanding, costs still outweighed revenue.

The new year was to be one of tumultuous change — as became apparent almost immediately with the dropping of Ron Hire. In what could have been the plot of a middling British crime caper of the period, it was found that his dealings had not always been, strictly speaking, legal. This was, not unnaturally, viewed as bad for the band's image. Derek Lawrence, speaking years later about his involvement with the 'mugs' who managed affairs, recalled what happened: 'There was a third one [along with Edwards and Coletta] and that was the 'H' of 'HEC', the managing company, who, in this time, had been arrested for selling forged paintings. So he got blown out'[1].

What can be said about this? Perhaps only that it was the 1960s...

In practical terms, it made little difference, since Hire had only ever been an investor who took no role in the running of the band. As far as that side of things went, 1969 began with the recording of a new album.

Looked at from the perspective of the 21st century, the pace at which Deep Purple churned out recorded material seems bewilderingly rapid. *The Book of Taliesyn* had not even been released in the UK as yet and was not to be so for several months, but, here they were, putting together another collection for the ever-hungry market. Given the time constraints, the overall quality of what was achieved was admirably high.

What can be said about this? Perhaps only that it was the 1960s...

The band had recorded some cover versions at a studio in New York during December, but they were deemed unsuitable for use and were unceremoniously ditched. Only three days after returning home, they went into De Lane Lea Studios in London. Lawrence was the producer, although this would be the last time, as he had, by his later admission, done everything that he thought that he could do for the band[2]. On January 7th, the sessions produced their first track in the form of the single, 'Emmaretta'. Famously named for the *Hair* cast member Emmaretta Marks, it is notable for other reasons, too. Not only was it the first original band composition to feature on an A-side, but it was the first single to be released in the UK ahead of America.

The hope, though, that it would repeat the success of 'Hush' proved to be forlorn and it floundered in the charts on both sides of the Atlantic. It is not difficult to see why. Driven by a wah-wah infused riff, it is not a particularly entertaining song. The tempo changes do little to dispel the feeling that it is all a bit too simple and forgettable. The truly banal lyrics ('Emmaretta / Did you get my letter? / I sent it to you...') do not help much. The review in *New Musical Express* summed things up perfectly: 'The standard of musicianship is unquestionably high, and Deep Purple's fire and urgency has a rawness and vitality that are difficult to resist. But the material is not outstanding by any means, so I can't be too hopeful about it'[3].

In the UK, it was backed by 'Wring That Neck', but, for the American release, a far more interesting original number was recorded. 'The Bird Has Flown' ranks with 'Mandrake Root' as a Mark I track that anticipates the band's future. Based around a relentless groovy riff, it is only a bit more fuzzbox distortion away from being worthy of consideration for inclusion on *In Rock*. The band seemingly came to realise this themselves. While 'Emmaretta' quickly faded into deserved obscurity, 'The Bird Has Flown' would go on to be recorded several more times — once, for a BBC session, by the Mark II line-up. There is no evidence that it was ever performed live, which is to be regretted. Indeed, an interesting counter-factual speculation might be to ask what would have happened had 'The Bird Has Flown' been released as an A-side? Would it have continued the good run in a way that 'Emmaretta' was not able to do?

Unlike its predecessors, the new album was written, as well as recorded, in the studio. This was mainly due to time pressures. Simper lamented the creative compromises that resulted: 'Recording was always a problem. We were always short of material, purely because of our schedule. The fact that we were always being chased by Tetragrammaton for material, we never had the luxury like most bands do now of saying, 'hang on fellas, we need a little bit of down time to just think about stuff and try and be creative'[4].

Despite such misgivings, the album stands apart from the first two in consisting almost entirely of original compositions. The lone cover version, of Donovan's 'Lalena', chiefly serves as a marker that the band were over cover versions. As a track, it is a pleasant enough listen, but is perfunctory. The creative ideas — for better or worse — that the band had brought to their earlier reinventions of 'Hush', 'Kentucky Woman', or even 'River Deep, Mountain High' and 'Help', are only lightly in evidence.

Another early indication of the current situation for the album was a song recorded on January 14th for another BBC session, which went under the title of 'Hey Bop a Re Bop'. Quite what this means is open to question, especially as the improvised-sounding lyric is all about waiting at a station for someone called Gloria. But it is, as the saying goes, what it is. A rather chaotic mix of organ and wah-wah guitar, the song still manages a strong bouncy beat that, all things considered, is reasonably infectious. It would appear on the final album in an amended, but not necessarily improved, form.

If it seems surprising that the band would present unfinished songs and unique recordings in BBC sessions (we have already seen that it was an approach taken by Mark II), they were not alone in doing so. Even into the 1990s and 2000s, bands would go into the studios at the BBC and use them as, to all intents and purposes, laboratories for musical ideas: it is one of the main reasons why BBC sessions are so valuable to the historian of popular music[5].

For the same session, the band recorded a version of 'Emmaretta' that was, if anything, slightly better than the one released on the single, as well as 'Wring That Neck', 'Hey Joe' and a Ben E. King and Bert Berns number called 'It's All Over'. The last of these exists only in this recording. In that the sole completed new song in this brief, but telling, set list was the single, it can be inferred that scant progress and been made on the album at this point.

Received wisdom is that the album is heavier than its predecessors, indicating better than anything they had done hitherto how the band were evolving into the Deep Purple with which people are most familiar. Listening back to it, this is not nearly as salient a feature as might be thought. Overall, the album puts into sharp focus the undeclared war between Lord's classical leanings and Blackmore's burgeoning hard rock sound. It was by no means where the controversy ended: the final battle would be fought not between tracks on a single album — it would be fought between whole albums. But the new material represented a major escalation of hostilities. Simper, in 1983, gave a blunt take on the situation: 'The reason the music lacked direction was Jon Lord fucked everything up with his classical ideas. Quite honestly, I don't think that Jon would deny it'[6].

In the classical camp, two tracks most stand out. The first, 'Blind', written by Lord, is a rather charming song that is ideal for Evans' voice and, for once, includes some nicely poetic lyrics. But it is played mainly on a harpsichord. As far as it goes, this is all to the good — the harpsichord is a lovely instrument in the right context. A Deep Purple album is almost certainly not the right context. Its inclusion, though, does argue for a couple of conclusions. The first is that the idea of sticking to a limited sonic palette, as demanded by hard rock — and which would be used to such magnificent effect on *In Rock* — was not endorsed by Lord. He clearly took the more prog rock line of allowing other instruments to be a part of the music.

The second conclusion to which 'Blind' leads us is more wide ranging: insofar as it could hardly be less hard rock if it tried, it implies that Lord does not seem to have felt that Deep Purple needed any one 'signature style'. He may have balked at Chris Curtis' roundabout concept as far as personnel were concerned, but a roundabout of musical styles and influences seems to have suited him just fine.

Exhibit B in the classical case is actually only two thirds of a track: the first two sections of this album's 'epic', the bizarre, yet wonderful, 'sort of concert' 'April'. At twelve minutes, it is the band's longest ever album track, although saying so is slightly disingenuous, since it would be more accurate to describe it as three tracks bolted together. The opening is an instrumental carried by Lord's twiddling organ and Blackmore's acoustic guitar. Vocals are confined to a few low-in-the-mix 'ahs' in the background. The section is an aural delight. Played with fabulous virtuosity, it evokes the beauty, mystery and melancholy of the English spring to perfection. It is a highlight not only of this album, but of the whole of Mark I's output and, understandably, can sometimes be heard, even today, as backing music to TV documentaries and the like. That it is very folky would make identifying it as a Deep Purple track difficult for any casual listener. An electrified solo from Blackmore does nothing to move it away from 'Albatross' territory.

That over, the most curious part of the entire album begins: Lord's orchestral description of April. Again, the music cannot be faulted for what it is. A richly imaginative composition, it, like the first section, does a good job of creating pictures in the mind of rain showers, blossoms and the weak, wan sunlight of the North at the tail end of winter. But, it is played entirely by a small orchestra. No member of Deep Purple contributes so much as a note. It is also, of course, pure classical, as opposed to classically influenced. 'River Deep, Mountain High' — the previous album's epic — may have had classical elements, but they were played by the band. Similarly, the strings on 'Anthem' accompanied the band — they didn't replace the band. The middle section of 'April' is simply a piece of classical music, played by classical musicians.

The other side of the debate is proposed by most of the rest of the album, but, if we are looking for *In Rock* DNA, we will only find it in one place. Almost all of the songs make use of a very dated-sounding wah-wah pedal.

'Chasing Shadows', which gets the album going, is typical. It is, on the whole, a really enjoyable track. Based around the rhythm section, it features some ace drumming by Paice, who uses every percussion instrument he can think of to get a groove going. Accompanying him is Simper, whose bass line is more-or-less the main riff. Lord and Blackmore come in over the top, providing power stabs and the occasional solo. It is fun and (no pun intended) pacey, but has little to do with where the band would end up going.

The first side concludes with 'Fault Line', a pointless, back-tracked prologue to 'The Painter', which is a redraft of 'Hey Bop a Re Bop', with different lyrics. Again, wah-wah dominates, although the basic rhythm is quite chunky and strident.

Side two includes a re-recorded version of 'The Bird Has Flown', retitled, for some reason 'Bird Has Flown'. This is an example of how the album is less heavy than it needs to be. The original is a Mark I gem, pounding, moody and intense. The new version is bloated and pretentious. For a start, the whole thing is overlaid with a very intrusive wah-wah track that serves only to attenuate its inherent power. It then fizzles out with an organ solo that is irrelevant to everything that precedes it.

If 'Bird Has Flown' embodies a certain creative confusion in the band at the opening of 1969, the same can be said of the third section of 'April'. Sounding not unlike 'The Painter', it just about meshes with the rest of the track (musically, it reworks elements of the first section). The lyrics (partly, it seems, based around the work of T. S. Eliot) are poetic, even if they do boil down to another tale of lovers being apart.

The one track that most accurately indicates the band's future trajectory is 'Why Didn't Rosemary?'. Despite it being claimed in the liner notes that it is based on an Otis Spann number and that it plays fast and loose with the format of twelve bar blues, the riff can also be heard on the Elvis Presley number 'Too Much' and it is very much a pilot for the type of songwriting in which the band would shortly engage. It is the one track on the album that makes much use of the fuzzbox, although the degree of distortion is relatively slight. It is also structured like the type of songs for which Deep Purple would become known. It has a main riff that drops out during the verses, of which there are two, followed by a guitar solo, followed by a final verse and a lead-out accompanied by more soloing. It even includes some of the keyboard work that, taken to an extreme, would later be heard in 'Hard Lovin' Man'. The lyrics are laced with a wit little in evidence elsewhere: they ask why the Mia Farrow character from the then-current film *Rosemary's Baby* didn't forestall the birth of the Anti-Christ by taking the recently-introduced female contraceptive pill. In an oblique way, this could be said to touch on issues of female empowerment not usually referenced by the band. With more distortion, more volume and a different singer, it can be imagined that 'Why Didn't Rosemary?' might have booked a berth on *In Rock*.

It would be easy to see the full album as a tired output from an increasingly tired band — recorded in a rush, unplanned, unrehearsed. Certainly, the packaging and release schedule (of which, more later) would suggest that. The album cover, irrespective of the controversies it caused in some American states, is no beautiful John Vernon Lord commission. The Hieronymus Bosch painting extract is rendered in black and white, not for artistic reasons, but because it was so reproduced by mistake and no one could be bothered to correct it. Equally, the album's title is — well, not a title. The album is simply called *Deep Purple* (only in later years, did it come to be referred to as 'Deep Purple III' or 'The Third Album').

The suspicion that inspiration had run out has much to support it. That would not be a fair comment on the music. For all of its schizophrenic qualities, the album stands up as surprisingly fresh, the growing presence of Blackmore in the songwriting coming through in some of the rockier material. Early reviews were by no means all dismissive. *New Musical Express* saw the mixture of musical styles as an asset, praising Lord's 'intricate and exciting organ playing', before concluding, 'the group have a tendency to be over gimmicky at times, but then anything original and entertaining runs that risk from time to time'[7]. *Melody Maker* afforded the album scant space, but the verdict was resoundingly positive: 'Plenty of evidence of real musicianship and original thought, even if there is a lack of immediate impact. Tasteful and beautifully produced music' [8].

The recording of the album was interspersed with a full programme of live performances. After a couple in the comfort zone of Scandinavia, the majority took place in the UK. In that the range of towns and cities covered was broad in geographical scope, they amounted to the band's first substantial tour of their home territory. Following the previous year's decidedly lacklustre assault on the home market, this can be seen as a statement of intent about where audience-building priorities lay. But, it must have all seemed like quite a come down for the band's members. Stops at such modest-sounding venues as Wolverhampton College of Technology on February 8th and Kay Club Milford Haven on March 1st[9] hardly compare with opening for Cream at Inglewood Forum.

Ian Paice highlighted the problem with booking the band in Britain, telling *Melody Maker*: 'We haven't been offered the money we want and, unless there is some sort of prestige attached, there is no point in doing the general run of gigs'[10]. Contrasting this with the band's situation in America, he went on: 'We have been given proper exposure [in America]. The Americans know how to push records. Over here, for example, nobody wanted to know about us on TV. We'd like to work regularly in the States — you have to have a proper financial basis to last in this business — but I don't think I'd like to live there'[11]. In the end, then, it all came down to money.

The set lists from that British tour are not easy to come by, but those from early Mark II shows, which still featured Mark I music, suggest that 'Shades' and 'Taliesyn' were most ruthlessly plundered for tracks that would work in a live setting. Apart from when done for BBC sessions, there is little evidence that songs from the self-titled album were ever performed live (despite 'Bird Has Flown' and 'Why Didn't Rosemary?''s obvious potential as crowd-pleasers). In part, this may have been down to a typically anarchic release pattern that afflicted the album.

In America, it came out in June, at roughly the same time that 'Taliesyn' finally hit the shops in the UK. In the UK, it was not released until September — by which time, the Mark I line-up was already history. If these were not, in themselves, enough to account for its initial commercial failure, more serious was the imminent collapse of Tetragrammaton. The major problem was that Deep Purple, for all that they were still only building a fan base, were by far the label's biggest act. As post-'Shades' and post-'Hush' releases struggled in the market, so did

Tetragrammaton.

Another issue was that the label was the home of the US release of John Lennon and Yoko Ono's *Unfinished Music No. 1: Two Virgins*, which came out in 1968. In theory, this should have been a guaranteed money-spinner, but it did not include any pleasant Beatles-style ditties, or even the type of music which would better characterise Lennon's later solo career — instead, it was a series of directionless improvisations of strictly limited appeal. Even more of an issue was the album's cover, which featured a photograph of the couple naked: because of it, EMI declined to have anything to do with it and it was criticised as pornographic in America, where many shops refused to stock it. In fact one pressing plant had its stock seized, which only compounded Tetragrammaton's woes.

By the second half of 1969, it was clear that Tetragrammaton were in big trouble. The days when members of Deep Purple could boast that they were receiving quarter of a million dollar advances from the label were long over. Money for pushing *Deep Purple* simply was not there and the album bombed.

At the start of the year, that was all still to come. More urgent was a growing rift within the band — not the one that might most be expected, given the musical differences that were becoming increasingly prominent. Rather, Blackmore was beginning to feel that the lead singer was no longer up to the job. It would be fair to ask why.

After all, for the type of music that the band was playing, he was as good a fit as any. His rich bass tones and ability to hold a note were what most of the songs needed. If, say, Ian Gillan had sung 'Blind' or 'Anthem', it is difficult to imagine that the result would be an improvement on what we have. Evans demonstrated an admirably dynamic range on such tracks, against which

Gillan's delivery would finish second best every time. It was with other, more and more important songs, that Evans was found wanting. He never sounded very comfortable singing 'Mandrake Root'; even on the album version, he is unable to really get to grips with the melody and the pounding backing against which it is set. The same can be said of 'Why Didn't Rosemary?', on which he holds his own, but he does not give anything like his best performance on the album. 'Listen, Learn, Read On' suffers from similar shortcomings: the spoken style simply does not suit him, despite the addition of resonant effects.

The heavier elements seemed to have had much to do with what was gracing Blackmore's turntable. It can be no coincidence that Led Zeppelin's first album was released in January 1969 — the very month that the recording of the Third Album got under way. Compared to Robert Plant's high-pitched screaming, wailing and shouting, Evans' crooning style must have felt like the most constricting of musical straitjackets. Then there was the ever-present spectre of Hendrix: how could Deep Purple ever hope to compete with him if the best that they could do was 'Shield' and 'One More Rainy Day'? It didn't matter that the studio recordings were failing to capture the energy of the band on stage — the studio recordings were all most people were ever going to hear...

Deep Purple may be a sonic stand off, but the would-be combatants are more extreme than on any other Mark I product: oh, you're going heavy, are you? Well, here's a full-on orchestra — how d'you like them apples? Unluckily for him, Evans was too closely identified with the camp that was slowly losing the fight.

When interviewed for a BBC documentary aired in the 1990s, Lord described how Blackmore broached the subject of a line-up change: 'We were recording our third album and Ritchie took me to one side and said something of the order of, 'Rod isn't cutting it and Nicky's bass playing is not what we need'[13].

The lazy way to look at this would be to see it as an example of the Machiavellian manoeuvring of which the guitarist has all too often been accused. But, as ever, there are two sides to the story. Evans had met, and fallen in love with, a young lady in America during the band's time over there and was now giving a good deal of thought to emigration. With none of the technology at his disposal that would make such a move not that big a deal today, any attempt to realise the plan would have been tantamount to resignation from the band. This perhaps contributed to a more general malaise that was afflicting him. By common agreement, he had lost interest in being Deep Purple's lead singer by early 1969. Simper spoke of how Evans had set his sights on Hollywood and harboured genuine aspirations of making it as a movie star (for the record, Evans has never appeared in any feature film)[14]. Ian Hansford, also spoke of how Evans was becoming detached and not putting in much effort[15]. Evans has a few songwriting credits on the third album, but it is far more Blackmore's show than either of its predecessors, regardless of the presence of 'April'. Ironically, Evans' decreasing willingness to get involved may have opened the door to Blackmore's growing influence, soon to be dominance: in this sense, could he be called one of the progenitors — admittedly unwitting — of *In Rock*?

Speculation aside, there was still a good deal of gigging to get through before any substantial changes could be made. Inevitably, this meant more American dates. Blackmore and a compliant Lord discussed their feelings with the management, but they still represented a minority within the band. Simper was sympathetic, but little did he know that the assassins' knives were being sharpened for him, too: his opinion did not really matter.

The plot all hinged on Paice's willingness to go along with it, or not.

Now, Paice, it must be said, is lauded — justifiably — as one of the nice men of rock. Spend five minutes in front of his *Drum Tribe* YouTube videos and you will gain all the confirmation you need of that. The man is a bona fide living legend. But his younger self displayed sometimes surprising levels of ruthlessness. Not only had he usurped Bobby Woodman without a second thought, but he was now being asked to turn on Rod Evans, his colleague from The Maze and, lest it be forgot, the one whose recommendation had secured him an invitation to audition for Deep Purple in the first place. Surely he would not agree to the jettisoning of his friend?

He agreed.

Without, it seems, needing to be much persuaded.

It is worth considering Paice's motives. On the one hand, his decision was simply a pragmatic acknowledgement of the nature of the rock music business. Paice has spoken frequently (he has, indeed, been quoted in this book doing so) about the need to grasp every opportunity that presented itself because it may not have presented itself again. As he was all too aware, there was little room for sentiment — especially at such a delicate early point in a band's life cycle.

On the other, any criticism of Paice's coldness would be made, again, with a heavy coating of hindsight. We may say that he callously prevented Evans from being a part of Deep Purple's future, but, when he did what he did, it was still Deep Purple's future: it was indeterminate at best. At that moment, all Paice would have known was that the stretch limos, top hotels and appearances on *Playboy After Dark* that had turned his head during the first American tour were not being matched during the latest British gigs. Besides, everyone involved with Deep Purple was used to frequent moves between jobs as bands evolved, or, more likely, failed. Was there any reason to believe that the same would not happen to Deep Purple sooner rather than later? Evans could find a front man slot somewhere — he had done so before. When Paice coolly threw in his lot with Blackmore and Lord, he had no way of knowing how any of their careers would pan out.

Anyway, a band majority secured, Evans' and Simper's fates were sealed — not that either of them knew it yet. But, with a new album to promote, the band were forced to carry on regardless, heading off on another American tour. Confusingly, the new album in question was not the third album, but *The Book of Taliesyn*. The tour was not particularly eventful. It criss-crossed the United States, taking the band from Alaska to Virginia to Oregon — and all over. Revenues were solid — they certainly dwarfed what the band was earning from British shows. Nevertheless, money was tight, mainly because of Tetragrammaton's financial woes. Frills were thus kept to a minimum, although not enough for Simper to be satisfied that money was always being well spent. Towards the end of the tour, the three conspirators made known their position to John Coletta, who raised no objections, viewing it as an artistic decision and, therefore, entirely the band's.

Little thought had been given to who would replace the departing members. Looking for advice, Blackmore contacted his former colleague Mick Underwood, who made his contribution to the chain of events that would lead up to *In Rock* by recommending Ian Gillan. Pushing the singer of your own band to become the singer of someone else's seems like an eccentric thing to do, but, by then, Episode Six were at a low ebb. The thirty thousand pounds-a-year deal had proven to be a chimera[16]. They were often booked by the BBC, but this gave a false impression of their popularity. Never ending touring was their standard modus operandi as they desperately attempted to drum up some public support. Increasingly bizarre stunts[17] were tried, but still the band remained niche.

Gillan — in a spooky echo of the difficulties being experienced by Deep Purple — blamed a lack of clear musical direction. The eclectic mix of cover versions that comprised most of Episode Six's releases was confusing: what type of band did they want to be? To Gillan, their best work was Glover's original songs, although a nervous record company was only prepared to contemplate their inclusion as B-sides. Even so, they were enough to cause some resentment among Glover's colleagues, who expressed their unhappiness at his status as 'band composer'. Gillan took a more far-sighted view and gradually became Glover's regular collaborator. This was to have profound consequences for Deep Purple and, ultimately, *In Rock*.

Lord and Blackmore went to see for themselves by attending an Episode Six concert at the inauspicious-sounding Ivy Lodge Club in Woodford Green, Essex. Suitably impressed, they set up a meeting to discuss terms. Gillan reports that, gauchely, he took cigarettes to offer around as a way to make the meeting run more smoothly[18]. He was speedily offered the job, despite, technically, there being no job to offer, which left the problem of filling the also-not-vacant bass player role. According to Gillan[19], he suggested his band mate Glover.

Glover does not seem to have been grabbed with the same enthusiasm as Gillan. As he explained: 'Paicey and Jon and Ritchie were masters of their instruments. We were amateurs by comparison. I went into the studio to play on a session for the song 'Hallelujah', and we were in different worlds. Paicey was the one who gave the nod to the others that I was an okay bass player. That night, Jon

Lord came up to me and said: 'We've had a little chat and we'd like you to join our band.' I said no.'[20]. A — perhaps misguided — sense of loyalty to Episode Six held Glover back. 'I felt an enormous amount of guilt,' he said, 'at leaving these people I'd slept in vans with, and struggled with and dreamed with and cried with'[21].

Gillan claimed to have spent the next few days trying to persuade Glover to change his mind — or, at least, make an informed, as opposed to emotional, decision. Finally, Glover opted to join and was admitted to the Purple family, with the unusual addition of a three month probationary period.

Evans and Simper meanwhile were blissfully ignorant of all this jiggery-pokery, believing that they were to play on 'Hallelujah'. By all accounts, elaborate ruses were used to keep them in the dark, including giving them incorrect times for rehearsals and recording sessions to ensure that they would not turn up until the new boys had left for the day. Simper later said that: 'It came to the ears of a very close friend of mine. He said, 'I've heard this rumour that you and Rod are leaving; they've got two new guys in'. I said, 'every time a band has a bit of success, you hear these rumours'. 'No', he said, 'I think it's true' and I just said 'that's rubbish'. I had that much faith in the band and that much faith in the guys I was involved with that I totally dismissed it'[22]. The surreal situation continued for some time, since Mark I had already-booked dates to fulfil. They continued to tour as Deep Purple, while a very different Deep Purple was gearing up behind the scenes. Evans' and Simper's last performance with the band took place on July 4th 1969 at the Top Rank, Cardiff. Mark I had lasted for just over a year.

Rather cravenly, the band prevailed on the management to break the news. As Lord himself pointed out, asking someone to leave a band is to attack that person's belief in their own ability and is thus particularly hurtful. Evans left, as we have seen, almost by mutual agreement. The same was not the case with Simper. Many have continued to maintain that his departure was both shocking and unnecessary.

Why it happened is still something of a mystery. He never did anything to suggest that he could not have played the sort of bass lines demanded by an *In Rock*. Indeed, he was one of those within the band who were pushing for a heavier sound. That Blackmore had become disillusioned with what Simper was doing does not, in hindsight, look out of character. Blackmore has always been impatient with bass players. It was he who, four years later, was to pull the same trick again with Glover, being the direct cause of his ignominious ejection. Bass players in Blackmore's Purple hiatus band Rainbow rarely survived for more than one album — with the ironic exception of a certain Roger Glover.

Simper's plight also had something to do with the new singer. It seems that Gillan was reluctant to leave his friend behind in Episode Six. Deep Purple were covetous of Gillan's talents and if firing the bassist was the price of benefiting from them, so be it. It was also lost on no one that Gillan and Glover had become a strong songwriting team. This, ultimately, was a deciding factor. Simper was a good bassist, but he only occasionally contributed anything to the creation of new material. Gillan and Glover — but Glover especially — brought a new creative dimension to the band. Their songwriting skills were a major asset, especially with cover versions now very much a thing of the past.

Shortly after Gillan and Glover joined, the band booked Hanwell Community Centre in order to do some jamming and, just maybe, generate some material for their next album...

In retrospect, the personnel changes proved to be spectacularly successful. To many of those who follow the band, this was the real start of Deep Purple — everything that went before was irrelevant: this certainly came to be Jon Lord's opinion[23].

Such a view, though, is grossly unfair. As we have seen, *In Rock* was not sculpted from nothing — its seeds were sown in the three Mark I albums and were not entirely undetectable in the output of the band's various members before they came together in the first place. True, the fuzzbox that would come to define the Deep Purple sound was not a strong presence, but it was increasingly forcing its way into the centre and heavy rhythms were definitely part of the equation.

It is valid to ask where the band would have gone next had the original membership remained intact. What would a fourth Mark I album have sounded like? It is, in all honesty, difficult to imagine. The third album may not have deserved much of the opprobrium to which fans have subjected it over the years, but it is something of a creative dead end. Another album along the same lines would not have been an enticing prospect.

Well, okay, but could Mark I have gone in a different direction? Blackmore was keen, but he lacked allies. Something else that Gillan and Glover brought to the party was a sympathy for the guitarist's vision — they, too, were anxious to experiment with a heavier sound. Soon after Mark II came together, Lord was to have possibly his greatest triumph, but thereafter, his influence on the band's output was severely diminished. It would take until 2002, when he left Deep Purple forever, for his creativity to return to the levels that it had been at during the Mark I period.

As for Evans and Simper: what became of them? The bassist continued to perform professionally, creating

Warhorse, a band that never quite got off the ground, despite their music doing a passable impersonation of Deep Purple Mark I. By the time I met him, in 2012, he was supplementing his pension by performing with The Good Old Boys, a tremendous pub band comprised of a number of old rockers who deserved considerably more celebrity than they were getting. He was also lending his talents to Nasty Habits, a Deep Purple tribute act that based its set around the three Mark I albums.

Curiously, he became the 'forgotten man' of Deep Purple, rarely mentioned and frequently left out from events that could, and should, have included him. He was nowhere to be seen at a concert to celebrate the life of Jon Lord, held at the Royal Albert Hall in 2014. Given that his history with Lord went back to before their Purple days, he was a glaring omission. More bafflingly, when Deep Purple were finally — belatedly — inducted into the Rock and Roll Hall of Fame in 2016, the citation did not include his name, even though the inductees were supposedly all of the members of the band's first three marks.

This may all have something to do with the circumstances of his leaving the band. Although the details are a little murky[24], the usual story is that, when offered either a cash settlement or a continued slice of the royalties pie, Simper took the former, thus exiling himself from the Deep Purple family forever. Presumably, whoever put together the Rock and Roll Hall of Fame citation believed this to be the case, or perhaps viewed him as a temporary member, or even a session player. Who knows? But, either way, he was not the only one to be snubbed, with several members of later marks losing out in similar fashion.

Rod Evans had an altogether different post-Purple afterlife. It may have struck the reader that, while almost everyone else involved with the band has been quoted extensively within these pages, Evans has not. He made few public pronouncements as Deep Purple's lead singer, but was positively chatty compared to how he has been since.

After a brief stint with the sort-of supergroup Captain Beyond, he dropped out of music, retrained as a medic and spent a number of years living an ordinary life in the USA. Persuaded to revive Deep Purple in 1980 (when the real band was on indefinite hiatus), he rather unwisely agreed to accept sole financial responsibility for an enterprise that had 'litigation magnet' written all over it. Nothing like a revival, it was essentially Evans and four musicians — who had no connection with the band — touring songs from marks with which he had not been involved. Forced to pay a colossal damages claim, he disappeared. Completely[25]. Nothing has been heard from him since. Some people presumably know where he is, but they are keeping very quiet. The rest don't know where he is or what he is doing.

None of this concerned the musicians who assembled at Hanwell Community Centre in 1969 intent upon creating something new and exciting. Fuzzbox at the ready, Deep Purple were leaving the classical stuff behind — almost. There was still one final legacy of the old days to be dealt with first...

Sculpting In Rock

8
CONCERTO

Interviewed by *Melody Maker* in August 1969[1], Jon Lord spoke about how pop music had grown up. No longer a three-chord twelve-bar bash, it was, in his opinion, developing into a sophisticated art form: 'The music has started to mean something and good musicians are to be found in abundance in the pop field. And the audiences have caught up, although the Great Beast that sells it to the public hasn't climbed up the hill yet.' He went on to talk about what Deep Purple proposed to do about it: 'I've never been with a group I thought could do it — until now. It won't be a case of doing a pop version of suitable classical themes; I am writing the whole lot from scratch. We will be doing a concerto. I know it sounds pretentious, but the last thing we want to be is pretentious, or edifying. I want people to have fun'[2]. Shortly afterwards, he told the *New Musical Express*[3]: 'I'm more interested in the pop, but there's a tremendous amount of enjoyable and emotional release in classical music. A lot of my generation don't believe this, but it's as exciting as the pop world. It's not stuffy.'

Lord's confidence did not match the reality of the situation in which the band found itself when those interviews were carried out. For a start, UK releases of Deep Purple's recorded material were in a chaotic state. By the time 'Taliesyn' appeared, the band that had made it no longer existed as such — and the third album was nowhere to be seen. In the event, Harvest, the EMI imprint to which Deep Purple had migrated, opted to release 'Hallelujah' at the same time as 'Taliesyn', placing one of the instrumental sections from 'April' on the B-side. In America, the situation was even worse, as Tetragrammaton's woes intensified. All of that is before the effort to which Lord had committed himself with his 'concerto' is considered: the statement that he was 'writing the whole lot' comes nowhere near describing what he had let himself in for.

As Lord acknowledged, the idea was not completely new. Love Sculpture — featuring the redoubtable Dave Edmunds — had produced a rock re-do of Khachaturian's 'Sabre Dance' in 1968. A superfast sweaty run-through, it has something of a Mark I meets 'Jam Stew' vibe to it. Keith Emerson, from The Nice was also moving in the same direction — he would go on to form Emerson Lake and Palmer (ELP) whose version of Copland's 'Fanfare for the Common Man' remains one of the best-known products of the classical-meets-pop sub-genre[4]. Deep Purple's label mates Barclay James Harvest were also about to start putting out music that straddled the line between classical and pop/rock. Their self-titled debut — released in 1970 — featured songs that were backed by a full orchestra.

None of these experiments amounted to a musical fusion as such. Playing classical tunes on rock instruments makes for interesting listening, but it cannot be called an exploration of the full potential of a marriage between the two styles[5]. Emerson, while still a member of The Nice, had given that a go, when he wrote the *Five Bridges Suite*. A love letter to Newcastle upon Tyne, it intertwined orchestra and rock band in ways intended to play to the strengths of both — just as Lord would go on to do with his 'Concerto'[6]. At only around eighteen minutes in performance, the suite is not especially ambitious — compared to it, Lord's writing is hubristic. The suite is also not wholly successful. Critics at the time, and since, have not been convinced that a synergy between the two styles was achieved[7]. Lee Jackson's vocals on the section entitled 'Chorale', moreover, sound distinctly out of place, being rather too shouty for an orchestral backing.

A much more committed effort was The Moody Blues' *Days of Future Passed* from 1967. Conceived as an album-length fusion of rock and classical, it does not really fit the description, since the band and the orchestra only play together during one section of the song 'Nights in White Satin'. Otherwise, it is a collection of Moody Blues songs stitched together by classical interludes composed and conducted by Peter Knight and realised by the London Festival Orchestra. The music plays without breaks, but it would be wrong to say that it adds up to a single work of art. In that sense, it provides context to Lord's composition, but, again, does not match it for scope and ambition.

While we are discussing rock musicians playing with classical forms, we should probably mention The Electric Prunes' bizarre, but charming, *Mass in F Minor* from 1968. Performed solely on electric instruments — although not, for the most part, by the band's members — it could best be described as ahead of its time.

It should not be forgotten, of course, that Lord had himself attempted a rock/classical fusion with 'April'. While the track ought — by rights — to be reappraised as a minor Deep Purple classic (albeit an oddball one), it was another in which rock band and orchestra were only on, at best, nodding acquaintance terms. Less a single piece of music than a medley of pieces united by a common theme (in the literary, not musical, sense), it served to demonstrate that rock and classical could live comfortably as neighbours, but not yet in the same house.

Classical composers adopting popular forms within their own work already had quite a long history. Shostakovich wrote a suite for jazz orchestra as early as 1938. Bernstein, in his score for *West Side Story*, among others, incorporated jazz and Latin rhythms into an aural tapestry that included more traditional symphonic sounds. In many respects, these were kin — distant and, to be sure, more respectable, kin — to Love Sculpture's 'Sabre Dance': they were about playing a different style within the conventions of the 'host' style. ELP's 'Fanfare for the Common Man' follows Copland quite closely, but it is still a piece of rock music. It has drums, bass, a strong rhythm. Shostakovich may borrow some of the conventions of jazz, but his work still sounds like a waltz.

Rarer was the bringing together of a rock band and an orchestra in order for each to do exactly what it was meant to do, but such as to harmonise with each other. Emerson tried it with only partial success on the *Five Bridges Suite*. The Moody Blues created the illusion of having done it. Jon Lord was to take it much further.

Lord said that the idea occurred to him several years before Deep Purple got together: if that is true, it would have been ripening in his imagination since the very earliest stages of his career. More immediately, it was a product of the remarkably fertile period towards the end of the life of Mark I; as Lord later said: 'In early '69, I went to my management and said, 'look, I've got this great idea, you know'. They said, 'who would write it?' and I said, 'huh, I would, you see?' They said, 'oh, terrific idea' and that was the last I heard of it for two or three months. Then one of the managers came to me and said, 'were you serious about this idea?' and I said, 'yes, absolutely' and he said, 'well, you'd better be because I've booked the

Albert Hall. Oh, and I've booked the Royal Philharmonic Orchestra, too, for September the 24th' — this being like April. I said, 'are you mad? Do you know how much work is involved here?"[8].

The timeline of the piece as finally composed is worth considering. Going by his own words, Lord's original proposal must have been made in around January or February of 1969. This would have been significant for a couple of reasons: firstly, that 'April' might have been either the inspiration, or a deliberate dry run, and, secondly, that the band that the concerto was written for was not the one that included Gillan and Glover. As a result, the 'group' elements of the concerto — albeit that they include some fuzzbox distortion — are far more Mark I than *In Rock* in style. Moreover, Lord would presumably have initially had Evans in mind as the singer for the vocal parts.

Not that any of that motivated the management to present Lord with the RAH fait accompli. For them, the reasoning was more cynical — the event would be a way to gain the band much-needed column inches in a Britain that still stubbornly refused to acknowledge their existence. If that meant burdening Lord with a nigh on impossible task, then it was a small price to pay!

The usual story is that the deal for the Royal Albert Hall and the Orchestra included the participation of the noted composer and conductor Malcolm Arnold, who Lord would go on to describe as the 'cornerstone' of the whole project[9]. Lord remembers things differently: 'At the point when I'd done about twenty pages of full score, somebody, I think, got slightly cold feet, having booked the Albert Hall and the orchestra and said — and the publisher said, 'can he actually do this, you know?' My management, who didn't know a crotchet from a hatchet, said, 'course he can, course he can, no problem at all!' They said, 'well, we'd better get some expert opinion' and the head of the publishing company was a friend of Malcolm, so this meeting was arranged: I walked in and there was this huge jolly man, saying, 'come here, let's have a look' and just grabbed the score out of my hand. Seven, eight seconds, said, 'yes, this will work very well' and flung it back at me'[10].

Arnold is another of the larger-than-life characters who populate this story. Born in Northampton, he, in common with many a rock star, disliked school, but was fortunate enough to receive home schooling. His growing love for music earned him a place at the London Royal College of Music, where the trumpet was his chief focus (he was a multi-instrumentalist).

From there, it would be tempting to say that everything was plain sailing. For sure, he composed over 500 pieces, including symphonies, dances and film scores — the best known being that for David Lean's classic, *Bridge on the River Kwai*. Among his prolific output were comic pieces, including one with the exotic-sounding title of 'Beckus the Dandipratt'. That he is not placed in the first rank of twentieth century British composers is a factor of his popular approach: loved by audiences (and, indeed, women), he was treated sniffily by a musical establishment controlled by elitists. This made him, though, the ideal collaborator for a bunch of long-haired rock musicians!

More ominously, he fought a lifelong battle against mental illness and alcoholism that manifested itself in suicidal thoughts and attempts to take his own life. At one point, many years after his Deep Purple adventure, he ended up homeless and was only saved from whatever disaster that could have led to by the pure chance of someone recognising him and setting him up in a house in Norfolk.

It was an ignominious fate for someone who did much to thrust classical music into the lives of those for whom it had always been something remote and exotic. Like Lord, Emerson and others, he, too, in his own way, brought genres together, combining the popular and the classical, as in his *Cornish Dances* of 1966. As he said, 'Music is a social act of communication among people, a gesture of friendship, the strongest there is'[11].

Not only did he give his seal of approval to the score, but, upon learning that no conductor had been engaged, offered to take on the job. 'In that two short minutes,' Lord later said, 'he changed my life'[12]. Arnold made another vital contribution in encouraging Lord to broaden the scope of the project. Initially conceived as just a single movement — which, on the strength of the finished work, would have been much the same length as the *Five Bridges Suite* — Arnold suggested writing a true three-movement concerto. It is this that really makes the 'Concerto' stand out from its peers and competitors. Had Lord's original plan been followed, the result would probably have been little more than 'April Revisited'. The 'Concerto' in its final form has scale, dimension, depth and development.

The small matter of Lord putting the hybrid in his head down on paper proved to be a Herculean labour. For him, there was little down time between gigs — every spare moment was spent slaving over keyboard and manuscript paper. This was an issue for him, but not for the rest of the band. It became an issue for them when he started to miss rehearsals and writing sessions: his attendance at Hanwell Community Centre during the gestation period for *In Rock* was by no means 100 percent, much to the chagrin of his colleagues. It might be posited that this was a cause of Lord becoming less active in songwriting later in the band's career; his absences facilitated the creative relationships that excluded him.

Lord's role in the band unquestionably changed. At the start of the composition period, he was still arguably the band's chief creative force. By the time that the piece was performed, things had moved on such that Deep Purple's music was being written primarily by Blackmore, Gillan and Glover: this was to cause more than merely artistic tensions.

It has been said that relations within the band became so bad that Lord threatened to quit. This is only partially true. It seems that such a low was reached, but not then and not over the 'Concerto'. Lord himself put the record straight on this: 'That came during the writing sessions for what became *Fireball*. We were down in Cornwall and my wife had just had a baby and I drove back in the middle of some writing sessions overnight from west Cornwall, before the M5 existed — horrendous journey — and picked up my wife and baby then drove them right back down again back into writing sessions. Twenty-four to thirty-six hours later, my new baby got a terrible cold because this place we were in was damp and awful and my wife just threw a wobbler and said I've got to go back to London. So I drove her back again and then drove back down again, thus missing two or three days of the writing sessions. They were not happy about that and rightly so, although perhaps they could have been a bit kinder given the circumstances. So a big argument blew up about that and I threatened to quit for some strange reason but, of course, it was just one of those moments: oh, fuck it I'm going to leave and walked out and slammed the door'[13].

Nonetheless, that the other members of the band were at best guarded in their enthusiasm for the 'Concerto' is well known. Even before it was performed, Blackmore was playing it down, describing it as 'purely a gimmick' and adding, drily, 'The RPO is interested in getting together with the group: I hear that one of the violinists has all our records'[14]. After-the-fact interviews confirmed that Lord received little support from his band mates during the composition period. Gillan has said that opposition came from, 'Ritchie, in particular... words were spoken to the effect that we were a rock band making a major album'[15]. In a much later interview, Blackmore gave more detail: 'We were a rock band. I couldn't understand why we kept playing with orchestras. It started to get up my nose... I was impressed with what Zeppelin did, and I wanted to do that kind of stuff, and if it doesn't take off we'll go and play with orchestras the rest of our lives'[16]. Glover's chief objection was that — in a repeat of his Episode Six experience — his songwriting contribution was being overlooked, as perceptions beyond the band were that Lord was not only the leader, but the chief, if not sole, writer.

The general attitude of the band's members towards the 'Concerto' can best be underlined by recounting the oft-told tale of how its vocal section came about. Following the usual practice, Lord left the writing of lyrics to the person who would have to sing them — Ian Gillan[17]. The problem was that, as the weeks went by, it became clear that Gillan was not writing them and the performance was getting ever closer. Lord would ask about work in progress on an almost daily basis, but, despite reassurances that they were on their way, no lyrics appeared. In the end, Gillan supposedly wrote them the day before the dress rehearsal, with Malcolm Arnold, in an Italian restaurant while the two imbibed large quantities of Chianti. Eschewing manuscript paper — or, indeed, any kind of conventional writing paper — Gillan wrote on a napkin[18].

At the 2014 Royal Albert Hall concert to honour Lord, Gillan showed this famous artefact to the audience, or, at any rate, he showed a napkin that might have been it to the audience: it didn't matter whether it was the real thing, because, like a holy relic, its power came from sources other than genuineness.

Other aspects of the 'Concerto' performance that were in the gift of the band and distinctly last-minute were the solos. Used to improvising, the band's members treated the 'Concerto' — in this respect, at least — like any other gig. Speaking of which, those continued while the 'Concerto' was being created in the background.

The punishing touring schedule did not pause to give Lord space in which to compose. The earliest Mark II performances, even on the rare occasions when they were recorded, were never released, but bootlegs have existed for decades, one of which appeared as *Kneel and Pray* in the early 2000s. This curio preserves the band's first appearance (of many) at the Montreux Jazz Festival in October 1969 and it is a fascinating document.

Recorded shortly after the 'Concerto' concert, it nonetheless, gives a snapshot of what the band were up to at the time. The first point to note is that it includes only two *In Rock* songs — actually, one-and-a-half if 'Kneel and Pray' is taken to be a work-in-progress. After that rough-and-ready opener, the concert settles into a familiar pattern of Mark I tracks and cover versions, with only a fairly straight account of 'Child in Time' lending novelty. 'Hush' gets a run out, as does 'Kentucky Woman' — the only extant recording of Gillan essaying the song, something he manages with reasonable success. A very long 'Paint it, Black' provides a vehicle for Paice's drum solo.

More interesting are the performances of 'Wring That Neck' and 'Mandrake Root'. The former is over twenty minutes long, the latter nudges twenty-five. To some extent, this reflects the band's paucity of performance-ready material: if you only have a few viable songs, extending the ones you have is a good way to fill up the running time of a concert. That said, even once the band had amassed a good quantity of material, lengthy improvisations would still be a staple of their concerts. In later years, 'Space Truckin'' would often last up to half an hour, having the instrumental section of 'Mandrake Root' tacked on to its end (on which basis, a Mark I song can be said to have continued in set lists up until the band's hiatus).

The recording demonstrates that the band developed their improvisation-heavy live style relatively quickly and stuck with it. It also highlights the durability of the Mark I songs, which were to continue to be performed in some form until the release of *Machine Head* — the second Mark II album, *Fireball*, was never extensively mined for live material.

Throughout August and September, the band travelled around not only the UK, but Belgium, the Netherlands, Germany and, inevitably, Scandinavia. In the few days leading up to the Royal Albert Hall engagement, the band played Malvern and Redcar — two English towns that are not conspicuously close to each other, or, for that matter, London. Where Lord got the time to write the 'Concerto' — much less the energy — is a mystery that would merit its own investigative book.

But, somehow, he kept his promise to his managers. He produced a score to the given deadline.

As completed, the 'Concerto' is, by any reckoning, a masterpiece. It is surprising that it and the studio album that followed it, *In Rock* (actually, the two studio albums that followed it), are not considered the band's creative apex — indeed, a creative apex for rock music as a genre. Why it isn't probably comes down to the types of people who constituted a group that did not really exist as yet, but would soon — Deep Purple fans. They were just not into classical music, or even prog rock, under which heading the concerto could just about be catalogued. They were heavy rockers, pure and simple. The direction defined by *In Rock* had room for experimentation within a strictly limited range. Playing classical music with orchestras was not part of the plan.

It should also be said that the band's achievements within the heavy rock genre came to be such as to wipe out anything else. *In Rock* would be a definitive, no-going-back-from-here, landmark, but the fact that the band came to be seen as 'that lot that did 'Smoke on the Water'' would deter most people from the deeper digging needed to uncover a *Concerto for Group and Orchestra* lurking in their catalogue.

Of this, it can only be said, 'more's the pity'. The 'Concerto' has been presented within these pages as the proposition in a debate, to which *In Rock* was the opposition, but that is to take a rather simplistic line. The 'Concerto' is, in and of itself, intended to embody that debate. The music is a discussion about how the two genres of rock and classical can peacefully co-exist, or even enrich each other. Combining the group and orchestra was not only practical, but thematic. As Lord said in 2011: 'It's a battle, then a truce and then a celebration — that's what the piece is, that's the three parts'[19].

The first movement (moderato — allegro) lives up to this description, orchestra and band being largely kept apart. The first seven minutes are orchestra only, a brooding, slightly ominous, atmosphere being built through the mixing of strings, timpani and booming brass. Crescendos, inventive dynamics and a melange of musical textures keep the interest high until some huge distortion-heavy chords announce the arrival of the group. The orchestra drops out as the band plays a heavy riff, enlivened with an early guitar solo. At the twelve minute mark, a call-and-response section between the group and orchestra leads to a brief flurry of dramatic orchestral music, before the group kicks in again with a delicate organ solo, behind which strings play as the group and orchestra begin to move together. Some unaccompanied soloing from the guitar takes the movement towards its climax, in which both ensembles are working together.

The second movement (andante) is probably the most crowd-pleasing, since it includes the vocal part. This comes in after around five minutes or so of primarily strings-based orchestral music, which has a lovely melancholy feel, only turning more jaunty as Gillan joins in. The vocal parts are divided into two, neither of which is a 'song' as such — just a part of the general flow of the movement, consisting of four brief verses without choruses. The first vocal part is melodic and subdued, a pleasant lead in to the second part, which comes a couple of minutes later and is much more passionate, featuring Gillan's soaring voice and a few of his trademark screams and whoops.

Those hastily-scribbled lyrics bear some consideration. For the first part, they are the sort of poetic-sounding nonsense that was standard issue for Gillan at the time: he sings of a 'sword in [his] hand' that can 'cut through the wood', while 'peace in [his] heart' serves to 'soften the mood'. It sounds fine, but is straight out of the 'Black Night' lyrical playbook. The second half, however, is more pointed. Bruce Dickinson, speaking in 2012, gave his interpretation, 'The words — you read the words — and it was Ian [Gillan] just crapping himself, going 'what is this all about? Suppose I fall flat on my face?'[20].

That is one way of looking at it. Another is that the lyrics convey Gillan's opposition to the whole project. He asks how he will know when to start singing his song, worries that 'they' (presumably the audience) will stand laughing at him and wonders what he will do 'when' — not 'if' — it all goes wrong. If the lyrics take a position, it is that a *rock 'n' roll* singer does not belong on a stage with an orchestra.

The vocals over, a melancholic, but beautiful, mood descends. The orchestra's parts have a genuine ache of longing about them, while the band contributes some blues and an organ solo that takes its cues from the classics. Some of the orchestral work is done by a small string ensemble, rather than the full orchestra, giving the movement nicely varied textures and dynamics.

The third movement (vivace — presto) is purely instrumental again. It is grand, with an epic sweep, carried by horns, timpani and Paice's furious drumming. The band and orchestra spend most of this section playing together, although an extended drum solo gives everyone apart from the indefatigable Paice a breather. Towards the climax, strings and percussion build tension, with Lord throwing in some heavy organ. By the end, band and orchestra are finally playing in unison, having resolved their differences and found a common ground in music.

Describing the 'Concerto', even in impressionistic terms, gives some sense of its scale and perhaps suggests why the band were so reluctant to involve themselves with it. Gillan's question, in context, was apposite: what would they do if it all went wrong? It is thus not surprising that it was a nervous Deep Purple that assembled for the concert's rehearsals towards the end of September.

In the event, such difficulties as there were came not from the rock 'n' roll side, but from the orchestra. Blackmore complained about the attitude of classical musicians: 'The orchestra was very condescending towards us and I didn't like playing with them'[21]. Gillan recounts a story of a female cellist standing up during a rehearsal and announcing that she refused to play with a bunch of 'second-rate Beatles'[22]. More entertainingly, Paice spoke of the difference between the orchestra — all classically-trained musicians — and the band, most of whom could not read music: 'Jon's got his full score there and there's Malcolm Arnold, the conductor, with his conductor's score and Ritchie's got his bits and I come in with this piece of paper, like this — torn out of one of those scrapbook things. With great sort of grandeur, I get my music stand and I place it — I stick it on with a bit of chewing gum. I can see the first violinist going, 'he can't read music — it's not going to work'. There was this belief that we wouldn't be able to play and it would be a catastrophe and what the hell were we doing fronting them, who were real musicians? That whole, you know, serious musicians against little pop people, you know?' On Paice's paper were such notes as, he said: 'First movement — hang around for seven minutes, listen for three big bangs, come in with first *rock 'n' roll* tempo, watch Malcolm, stop — and it went through the whole thing like that'[23].

The element that brought everything together was Arnold. Lord spoke of how nothing could have been achieved without him: 'A cello player came up to me and said, 'excuse me, Jon' — no 'maestro', or anything like that, but I wasn't expecting that — just Jon, 'what you've written here, it's impossible'. And I was just about floundering to say, 'oh dear', and Malcolm came up and said, 'we'll sort that out: just take that note out and bow it like this and you'll be fine', sending the guy back into the orchestra and leaving me open-mouthed with gratitude because I wouldn't have known how to deal with the situation'[24].

Lord went on: '[Arnold] was everywhere. He was down in the orchestra, putting notes right. He was helping with bits of the writing. [The rehearsal] was probably the most terrifying day of my life... and Malcolm was this wonderful, benign, roly-poly chap, who went around distributing bon mots and friendship and hugs and 'come along, everything's going to be fine' and that sort of thing and, of course, the band were terrified... The orchestra were treating us pretty shabbily at first, I must be honest. Malcolm was the barrier between them and us, or the translator, if you like, and his famous line, which he stamped his foot and banged the podium — the lectern — and said, 'no, no, no, no, no, this will not do — you've got five young men here playing their hearts out and you're playing like a bunch of... asterisks — Old English"[25].

A TV documentary crew captured a brief exchange between Lord and Arnold during a lull in the rehearsals — it not only conveyed their satisfaction at what they were achieving, but indicated the genuine affection and respect that they had for each other[26]:

> ARNOLD: What's it feel like, playing with us squares?
> LORD: Wrong word! Wrong word! It's great, actually. I mean, the first rehearsal the other day, I sat down here and was looking over there [at the orchestra] — it's been very exciting.
> ARNOLD: It has for me!
> LORD: I hope the concert itself is as exciting as the rehearsals.
> ARNOLD: It will be more exciting...

Major problems during the rehearsals occurred around timings. The eighty-plus members of the orchestra needed very precise instructions, which they obtained from their conductor, whereas the band, used to playing along to a beat set by their drummer, could afford to be looser. The orchestral score was very meticulous and detailed, whereas the band's solos were mostly improvised, again causing cuing problems. Somehow, it all came together — mainly, if Lord is to be believed, because of Arnold. As Lord related, the conductor's other famous quote (on top of the 'bunch of whatevers' one) was words to the effect: 'We're making history tomorrow. We might as well make music, too'[27].

The actual performance began with the orchestra alone playing Arnold's *Symphony No. 6, Op. 95*. A recently-completed piece, it fitted in with the overall concept of the evening in consisting of movements influenced by jazz saxophonist Charlie Parker as well as different styles of pop music. The band then had their own 'solo' spot, playing 'Hush' (presumably chosen as their biggest hit to date), 'Wring That Neck' (which was extended, but not to the gargantuan length that would become the norm at early Mark II concerts: it was present, no doubt, because it was the closest thing the band had to their own piece of classical music) and, perhaps most excitingly of all, 'Child in Time' (a not-yet recorded indication of where the band were headed). All three were beautifully performed, especially by Gillan, whose soaring notes on the new song defied description.

These 'introductions' done, the 'Concerto' took over. For all of the worries, concerns, frictions and potential disasters, the performance was nigh on immaculate. Blackmore was so into it that he kept one of his solos going for a few bars longer than strictly allowed by the score. Gillan was passionate and earnest in his singing and Paice, makeshift notation notwithstanding, did not skip a beat. Watching the film of it confirms that, at no point, did any member of either the group or the orchestra ever seem to be less than one-hundred percent committed.

The management's desire for the event to be a way of raising the profile of the band was fulfilled in spades. Most immediately, the huge Albert Hall audience was clearly delighted. Reviews in the following days were also mostly very positive. For *New Musical Express*, the concert was, 'a resounding success', not only for the critic, but for, 'the large crowds of youngsters and older folk present'[28]. Moreover, the review continues, 'At the end of the opus, the audience went wild. It was an act of spontaneous pleasure, the like of which I haven't witnessed since England won the World Cup'[29]. So there you go! *Melody Maker* were equally ecstatic, praising the audience for mainly comprising, 'those rather nice people — classical hippies'[30] and commenting that: 'The timing was brilliant and Jon's fellow members of Deep Purple seemed quite at ease and not in the least hesitant as they matched their sound with the Royal Philharmonic Orchestra'[31].

The mainstream media, finally waking up to the band's existence, was similarly filled with positive ratings: the *Sunday Times* called the event, 'joyous and impressive', *The Guardian* went with 'impressive' and *The Daily Telegraph* described Lord as, 'clearly a natural musician'. Even the *International Herald Tribune* got in on the act, judging the blending of rock and classical, 'an astonishingly happy communion'. The TV coverage didn't hurt either!

It is a moot point as to how far the band's suddenly-elevated profile gave *In Rock* a tail wind that carried it to the heights that it reached. On the one hand, Deep Purple were 'hot' after the concert and it might be expected that the public were eager to get their hands on their next release. On the other, that next release, as far as the UK was concerned, was the third album, which sank like lead. With the benefit of our old friend hindsight, Gillan, speaking ahead of the first revival of the concerto in 1999, saw a connection: 'I was very impressed by [the 'Concerto'], actually. I've always been impressed by Jon Lord. I remember going around to his flat and seeing manuscripts all over the walls and the carpets — which subsequently got lost, by the way. But there was a sort of air of ambivalence about it at the time — we didn't realise until afterwards — quite apart from the musical value — that in fact it got a lot of publicity for the band and it probably did a lot to help *Deep Purple In Rock* get the recognition it did"[32].

Back in 1969, band members adopted a more determined stance against further crossover pieces. Blackmore, speaking to *Melody Maker* in November of that year, had it put to him that rock/classical crossovers are 'unnecessary'; his answer was unequivocal: 'I'm inclined to agree. Although I felt that the concert was a success and this was only an experiment. It isn't the direction that we, as a group, are going in at all'[33]. Even Lord, referring to the 'mixed media' approach said, 'It became a kind of musical cult instead of a musical experiment in a different level. I'm very much into what the group are doing now and I think that our policy of gigging almost anywhere in the past six months up and down the country has really got through. What we are doing now has always been at the root of our music'[34]. Talking to *Disc* magazine some months after the concert, he asserted that, as a group, Deep Purple had decided not to do any more classical crossovers 'for the time being'[35].

Were Lord's colleagues right to take so high-handed a view of his efforts? It would be too easy to see their attitude as mean-spirited and, on the part of Gillan and Glover, ungrateful, since they had — through no efforts of their own — been granted a stage the like of which they had never trodden on before. But the worry that the band could well find themselves touring with orchestras ad infinitum was genuine and, frankly, understandable. In the wake of the concert, they were perceived as a prog band, or even art rockers: it was not what they — in particular, the new boys — had signed up for. They wanted to play *rock 'n' roll*! In many respects, the 'Concerto' was a Jon Lord solo project of which they just happened to be a part: Gillan's very brief — and last-minute — lyrics aside, no other writer is credited apart from Lord. Whether the string players of the Royal Philharmonic wished to recognise it or not, he was the maestro. The rest of the band cannot really be blamed for treating the whole thing as a deviation from their true path.

Ironic, then, that, not only has the concerto's stature grown over the years, but that there was a 'Concerto Part Two'. *The Gemini Suite* is best known as Lord's first proper solo album, released as a studio recording in 1971 and featuring such stars of the day as Yvonne Elliman on vocals and Albert Lee on guitar. The London Symphony Orchestra, conducted again by Arnold, provide the classical parts. Glover and Paice pop up to contribute solos, but it is not a Deep Purple project.

Except that it was...

Commissioned by the BBC with the intention of recreating the success of the 'Concerto', the first performance took place in September 1970 at the Royal Festival Hall, with Deep Purple accompanied by the Light Music Society Orchestra conducted - obviously - by Malcolm Arnold. Many fans of the band will be blissfully ignorant of this occasion, largely because that is what Blackmore intended. He, along with Gillan, had to be dragged kicking and screaming to the performance, which they only agreed to on the basis that there would be one performance only, that there would be no publicity and that it would be broadcast on radio and then quietly forgotten. By this point, the band were in a much stronger position than they had been the previous year. No longer has-beens, or, more likely, never-weres garnering less and less public interest, they had a high profile based on a sustained chart assault led by a well-received album and a hit single. With the 'Concerto', they had had nothing to lose — now they had an image and a reputation. Although the concert was recorded, it was not officially released until 1993, and only then as a present-to-hardcore-fans novelty.

Concerto

Lord's take on the whole business is interesting for what it says about his evolving role within the band: 'The BBC came to me and said, 'would you write another one?' And of course I was thrilled to be asked to write for something as auspicious as the BBC; they thought it was a worthwhile experiment and I went to the rest of the band and said, 'I've been asked to write another one would you like to do it?' And they said, 'well, not really', but the management somewhat talked them into it. We did do it live but by that time they were really, 'we don't want to do this', and I, while being unhappy they didn't want to do the recording of it, was still at peace with myself and with them over the dichotomy, the difference between us'[(36)].

The piece is called *Gemini Suite* because it is structured around the personalities of the members of Deep Purple, who are coded by their star signs, hence 'Gemini' — although this could also have been an acknowledgement that the suite is essentially a twin of the 'Concerto', the structure of which it borrows almost exactly: three movements, vocals confined to the central one, the vocals consisting of two parts with different melodies that are not discrete songs. The movements are designed to be showcases for each member of the band, but that does not really come across strongly. It is mainly a classical work, the band being very much in the background. Blackmore's fuzzbox-infused guitar part is jarringly at odds with the orchestral sounds that accompany it — only during a run in which he plays alone does he sound like he is having any fun.

On the surface, the lyrics are no longer even as mildly coy as those on the 'Concerto' — they seem to be a public admission that Gillan wants out. They begin with orchestral backing as the singer wishes that he wasn't there making what he calls 'silly sounds' as part of a 'funny show'. Only when the band kicks in does he admit to enjoying himself, since he is now singing *'rock 'n' roll'*. At one point, he longs to be drinking a 'glass of ale' instead of standing on that stage.

It is surprising, then, that they were written by Lord. What was he thinking as he drafted them? Were they a spiteful form of revenge – making the singer seem petulant and antagonistic to show up how he had reacted to the whole crossover experiment? That would have been out-of-character. More likely is that he was doing what he set out to do – reflect Gillan's personality in the composition. He knew that the singer was a rock 'n' roller at heart and put words to that effect in his mouth. By this interpretation, the lyrics demonstrate empathy and a desire to not let disagreements over music get out of hand: Lord is saying, 'I understand how you feel'.

Lord himself does not seem to have taken things entirely seriously, as he wanders off-score to play a few notes of Gershwin's 'Rhapsody in Blue' during his organ section.

To be sure, there are plenty of positives. Gillan — for all his disgruntlement — gives a beautiful performance, his singing reaching the heights of his best ever renditions of 'Child in Time'. The integration of band and orchestra is arguably more subtle than on the 'Concerto': whereas on the earlier piece, the two ensembles rarely played at the same time, they do so throughout *Gemini Suite*. And the classical pieces are achingly lovely, especially the string-led opening to the second movement.

The main problem, though, is that the band's sound had metamorphosed since the 'Concerto' and was that of the *In Rock*-promoting tours that were their workload for the rest of that year. Plainly improvising, the band produce heavy, often dissonant, noises that are fantastic as part of a wildly over-extended 'Mandrake Root', but do not often cohere into distinct melodies here. In short, the heavy rock to which the band had dedicated themselves just does not work as well with an orchestra as the Mark I style of music that had filled the Albert Hall on the night of the 'Concerto'.

Had *Gemini Suite* enjoyed more prominence, would it have detracted from the success of the 'Concerto'? It is tempting to answer, 'yes'. Sequels are not always needed. Sometimes, a work of art is best left as a brilliant and unique expression of its creator's imagination. So it is with the 'Concerto'; *Gemini Suite* comes close to cheapening it. The later work's obscurity is to be thanked for preventing it doing too much reputational damage to the work that preceded it.

The *Gemini Suite* is not to be entirely dismissed, but it should be put into context. The 'Concerto' was a triumph and ought to have been left at that. The final word on it — at least here — should perhaps go to Lord, reporting a conversation with Arnold: 'Just before I left [after the performance] I went over to [Arnold] to say goodbye and I sat down next to him and he said, 'we bloody showed them that night, didn't we?' I said, 'yes we did, we did'. He said, and you know, he looked around and beckoned me. I said, 'what?' He said, 'you know your singer?' I said, 'yes'. He said, 'he's got a dick like a donkey"[37].

9
SUPERSTAR

The album of the 'Concerto' was released in America on December 20th, 1969, thus becoming Mark II's first full-length release, although the fact that it was technically 'live' means that it is often disregarded when chronologies of the band's works are compiled. Still, it was the Gillan/Glover era's first major recorded output, which puts into perspective the reservations of Blackmore et al about doing it at all: the potential for the public to suffer confusion about what the band stood for was very real. The whole concert was not represented on the album[1], merely the 'Concerto', the second movement of which was split between the two sides — those were the days when running times were strictly determined by what could be fitted on to twelve inches of vinyl. The front cover imitated those of classical releases of the day, with a simple, informative, font and a photograph of the band sitting in an otherwise empty Royal Albert Hall. Reviews were mixed, the critic from *Melody Maker*, for example, wryly stating that: 'Lord describes critics in his sleeve note as 'necessary, but slightly archaic, appendages to the scene', so I'll go no further in discussing the actual music. Anyway, the man himself says it's only intended to be 'fun''[2].

What was a beginning for Deep Purple was an ending

for others, specifically, the owners and employees of Tetragrammaton, which finally collapsed in early 1970 under the weight of its failure to sign any other successful artists. The 'Concerto' album was distributed in America by the label, but it was the last Deep Purple release for which that was the case. It would go on to be re-released by the band's new American label, Warner, the following year.

It might be thought that that was that for classical crossovers, the *Gemini Suite* notwithstanding, but the 'Concerto' had an unlikely afterlife in the form of one more performance, albeit abridged, that took place in August 1970 at the Hollywood Bowl. Arranged by Warner to publicise the only 'legacy' Deep Purple album that they were putting out at the time, it was, if reports are to be believed, even more successful than the original.

Accompanied this time by the Los Angeles Philharmonic Orchestra, the band faced many of the same issues that had plagued the rehearsals in London. Lord spoke of, at first, sensing the hostility of the 'proper musicians' in the orchestra to the 'long haired freaks' that they were accompanying. But a rapprochement was, again, reached, leading, as before, to mutual admiration: 'On the Tuesday rehearsal, things began to click a bit better,' he said, 'One of the violinists beside me was really getting into it, and muttering, 'Yeah, far out' and such like to me. Lawrence Foster, the conductor, was really great and worked hard to whip everything into shape. And at the end of 'Concerto' when I asked the orchestra to rise and take a bow, well, they almost fainted. I don't suppose they expected me to know the correct 'classical' etiquette'[3].

Interestingly, it was not only Lord who came out of this event particularly well. The *New Musical Express* mentioned how, 'Hollywood found what it's been looking for, for ages — a new guitar hero in the shape of Ritchie

Blackmore. One critic summed him up by describing him as having 'double the technique, twice the speed and half the flash of Albert Lee'[4]. Furthermore, 'Little Ian Paice came in for some nice praise from the *Encino Chronicle's* noted music critic, Denis Rosoff, who described him as being 'the most controlled, most interesting drum soloist ever heard at the Bowl'[5]. Clearly, the management's plan to use the 'Concerto' as a way to get the band's name around was working on both sides of the Atlantic — even if it was to the annoyance of band members now well into the *In Rock* era.

It is ironic, then, that Gillan — for all of his obstructiveness over crossover pieces — actually found himself involved with another project that combined rock music not only with an orchestra, but with musical theatre. If he ever suffered from delusions of grandeur, they found some justification when he was offered the chance to essay the title role on the original album recording of *Jesus Christ Superstar*.

The show, as need hardly be said, was written by Tim Rice and Andrew Lloyd Webber — whose backgrounds were very different from those of the members of Deep Purple. Rice was an old boy of the exclusive private school Lancing College in Sussex, who had opted not to apply for university and had instead drifted around for a while in that way that only seems to be possible for people from relatively privileged backgrounds. He worked for a law firm, spent a year studying at the Sorbonne in Paris and generally marked time while searching for a vocation. For his part, Lloyd Webber followed Westminster School with an abandoned stint at Magdalen College, Oxford, before attending the Royal College of Music.

The two met in 1965 and immediately got to work on their first musical, *The Likes of Us*, which, setting a pattern for their collaborations, was the story of a real life character, in this instance, a social housing reformer. It was not produced — at least, not until many years later — but, realising that they were an effective team, Rice and Lloyd Webber pressed on with a follow-up, *Joseph and the Amazing Technicolor Dreamcoat*. Based, this time, on an Old Testament story, the piece has been often performed as a stage show, but was initially more like an oratorio, created to be recorded and listened to, rather than watched. It was an instant success, its pop music stylings (including a Pharaoh who sounds distinctly like Elvis) setting it apart from most of its generic peers.

Emboldened by this early hit, Rice and Lloyd Webber began drafting the similar, but far more ambitious, *Jesus Christ Superstar*. Rice, the lyricist and book writer, has said that he was inspired by a line in Bob Dylan's 1964 song 'With God On Our Side' that questioned the role of Judas Iscariot in the story of Christ's Passion[6]. Indeed, the finished piece is far more Judas' story than Jesus'. From the opening number 'Heaven on their Minds' to the climax from which the show takes its title 'Superstar', the main theme is Judas' interpretation of Jesus, rather than Jesus' deeds per se. It is, moreover, a resoundingly secular story. It depicts no miracles, no Resurrection and God is conspicuous by His absence — indeed, one of the standout songs, 'Gethsemane', deals with God's apparent unwillingness to do anything particularly Godlike.

Originally conceived as a theatre project, Rice and Lloyd Webber again found securing backing difficult, so the thought began to take root that it could be a concept album instead. The climactic 'Superstar' was written first as a sort-of pilot to be released as a single. Interestingly, Lloyd Webber came up with the melody in a restaurant on London's Fulham Road and noted it down on a napkin[7]: my next book will be on the role of napkins in rock crossover compositions.

138

Rice knew the singer Murray Head and offered him the chance to sing Judas' part. The recording was done at Olympic Studios in Barnes, London, featuring, at great expense, Head, a full orchestra, the Trinidad Singers (on backing vocals) and, providing the *rock 'n' roll*, Joe Cocker's house musicians The Grease Band.

The single was a sensation upon its release on 21st November 1969. In the UK, it, like the music of Mark I before it, received vital exposure on David Frost's chat show. Abroad, it rocketed to the tops of a number of charts, giving momentum to the idea of recording the whole story.

It was at this point that Gillan entered the frame. As Rice put it: 'I had a meeting at Andrew's flat — I remember — with Tony Edwards and we tried to give an impression of what we were trying to do and of course he'd heard the single with Murray and we said, 'we want someone who can match Murray, who's got a great rock voice and it's a rock thing and rock, rock, rock'. And Tony said, 'I think I've got a voice for you'. He went off and he came back about an hour later with a tape of Ian Gillan singing on 'Child in Time', I think, off *Deep Purple In Rock*. We said 'this guy's brilliant, we'd love him to do it' and we met Ian and Ian did it — we were quite surprised. We kept thinking, he's going to think that we're not very cool'[8].

Gillan supplies more detail: 'They had had a hit record with the song 'Jesus Christ Superstar', which was kind of a pop hit, but the opera hadn't been written. When it was, I got a call from Tim Rice, who had heard me singing with Deep Purple and had said, 'you know, we'd like you to play Jesus and can you do that?' I said, 'well, I'm kind of busy at the moment — we're working every day next week' and he said, 'we've got a studio booked for Wednesday morning, can you do that?' I said, 'we've got a gig in the evening, but that would be fine'. So, I went round to his apartment with

Andrew Lloyd Webber. They were — didn't give me the music, but the lyrics. He said, 'Andrew will play the tune for you. What we'd like you to do is sing it in your own way, to improvise, stretch out a bit, like you do with Deep Purple'. Andrew looked over his shoulder and said, 'yes, yes, yes, but not too much'. I kind of knew where I was headed. It was fantastic, because it was such a beautifully written tune'[9].

Gillan's account skirts over a few vital details to do with the writing of the whole show. Story-wise, it recounts what happens to Jesus during his last seven days on Earth, from His entry into Jerusalem to the Crucifixion. Gillan is right to call it an opera, rather than a musical, since it is sung through, with no spoken sections, or even much that could be called recitative. Instead, it consists of a number of separate songs of varying degrees of complexity. Some, such as 'Trial Before Pilate' are essentially dramatic scenes set to music, with characters and chorus interacting and whole sections consisting of non-verbalised action. Others, such as 'I Don't Know How to Love Him', are straightforward songs, comprising verses and choruses: they often describe characters' states of mind, but have no other dialogic function within the story.

While never less than entertaining, *Jesus Christ Superstar* is not without its flaws[10]. The first half is the less interesting, with songs such as 'Simon Zealotes' contributing little to the plot. Lyrically, the show also mostly lacks the depth of Rice and Lloyd Webber's later magnum opus, 'Evita'. Clunkers that would make even Emmaretta blush pop up here and there ('Always hoped that I would be an Apostle — knew that I could make it if I tried'), although Rice's characteristic wit is much on display ('If you'd come today, you could have reached a whole nation / Israel in 4BC had no mass communication').

From a musical perspective, Lloyd Webber has stated

that he would not take the same approach if he could go back and do it all over again: 'Of course I would write such a piece differently now. The thing that I hope does come through theologically even now is the great climax of the whole first act, the song 'Gethsemane,' which is very much Jesus' moment'[11].

This comment perceptively references two truths about the show. Firstly, that the music — as with all good rock records of the time — is not without its share of repurposed older material, the tunes for both 'I Don't Know How to Love Him' and 'Herod's Song'[12] having been written for other projects. Secondly — and more importantly — it sites Jesus within the narrative, hinting at why Gillan's casting was so inspired. The eponymous hero is multi-dimensional — not least in that His original is a figure of devotion for people all around the world. Within the narrative, He has to convincingly convey two traits. On the one hand, He must be a man, who is filled with doubts and contradictions ('What's the Buzz'/'Strange Thing Mystifying'), who questions God's plan ('Gethsemane'), scorns the possibility of His message having any durability ('The Last Supper'), loses His temper at the desecration of the Temple and tells sick people to leave Him alone and 'heal themselves' ('The Temple').

On the other, He needs to be iconic and aloof, a man who could convincingly be mistaken for God. He needs, in other words, to be someone who can stand on a stage in front of thousands of people, with sufficient charisma to hold all of them rapt, while making each one think that they know him personally. He needs, then, to be a rock star, a superstar — or, to give such a person a name, Ian Gillan. Blackmore emphasised this: 'He had the scream, he had the look. Ian had this presence. He was also doing *Jesus Christ Superstar*, which was excellent'[13]. This is why casting the show has not always been easy[14]: the Jesus is all too often either too human, or too divine. Striking that delicate, almost impossible, balance between the two extremes can only be done by the rarest of performers.

Of the recording, Gillan has said: 'I did the whole album in three hours that morning, at which point, Tim, at the end, not the beginning, said, 'I'm sorry to have to tell you that we've run out of money', he said, 'so we can't pay you'. Oh, right, okay. He said, 'would a royalty be acceptable?' Yeah, okay. So he said, 'how about a penny a record?' I said, 'yeah okay, that'll do'. The only thing I had trouble with was the sayings from the cross because you need a little acting experience to deliver those. I was overselling it and it sounded ridiculous. So I went back for another half an hour session to do that'[15]. During the additional session, Rice gave Gillan the advice to think of Christ as an historical character, rather than a Messiah: it was all the direction required. Gillan also claimed that, while making the album, the engineer pretended that he had fumbled the recording of the orchestra and asked them — to their understandable dismay — to play their parts again: it turned out that this was simply a ruse to allow for double tracking without the need to pay a second fee![16].

Following the album's release in October 1970, Gillan was asked, perhaps only semi-seriously, to reprise his role in the film version. He went to Shepperton Studios to meet with Norman Jewison, the director. It seems that it was no more than a courtesy visit. Gillan's demand for an — for 1970 — outrageous fee of a quarter of a million dollars, plus payments to the rest of Deep Purple for the duration of the shooting, were way beyond the resources of a relatively low-budget production. All of the roles were recast, except that of Mary Magdalene, which went to Yvonne Elliman, who had played it on the concept album. Gillan explained his reasoning as part of a more wide-ranging interview: 'I didn't think about it for more than a half hour. Here I was, in Deep Purple, the band I always dreamed of playing with. I wasn't going to jeopardise it for a run in the West End or twelve weeks on location filming the movie... Asking the rest of the band to stop working for three months would have been a problem'[17].

Irrespective of what happened in other media, the album went on to become a phenomenon, selling millions of copies, which no doubt earned Gillan many multiples of the reneged-upon two hundred pounds that he had been promised for doing it. Rice has spoken of the album's importance: 'Whenever they discuss great rock albums of the '70s, it's never mentioned and it was one of the biggest sellers of all — and it is rock, but it's perceived as a corny old musical'[18]. Rice pointed out that *Deep Purple In Rock* was a big hit, but 'Superstar' was even bigger. 'We were very lucky to get Ian,' he added, 'but I think he was lucky to get us, frankly. You know, it was just great timing'[19].

The stage show that grew out of the album was era defining. For a long time, it held the record for longest-running musical in London's West End. Productions around the world spawned a mixture of notoriety and admiration. Credited with inspiring young people to take an interest in religion, the show was also perceived as anti-God, anti-Semitic, blasphemous — the usual cocktail of 'anti's. It was protested against in various countries, some protests turning violent.

The film version, by contrast, ended up being a damp squib. Far from the glamorous, glitzy, rock piece written by Rice and Lloyd Webber, it was framed as the tale of a small gang of hippies putting on a production in the desert. The bleak, depopulated, settings established a tone of grimness where wonderment would have been more appropriate. Ted Neeley gamely screamed his lungs out as Jesus, but he lacked the charisma of Gillan.

For a long time, Gillan's involvement in the show

was one of those Deep Purple factoids of which many fans were, at best, only dimly aware. Overshadowed, like everything else, by 'Smoke on the Water', it was rarely referenced[20]. In fairness, it was not a Deep Purple project — despite Gillan's part in it being predicated on his membership of the band — but its proximity to *In Rock* makes it a compelling footnote to the band's history.

More recently, Gillan has been readier to discuss it, probably in response to its growth in popularity and significance. This no doubt surprised the man himself. All of his actions at the time suggest that he had no expectations that it would have more than a short lifespan. It seems that, not for the first time, Gillan's intuition for what would last and what would not was exposed as less than accurate.

A couple of the earliest publicity photos taken on 24th September 1968 at Pictorial Press office, Fleet Street, London.

Biggin Hill Air Display, 13th May 1967
(Wendy Ford / Nigel Lees Collection)

Episode Six was gigging regularly from 1966 and neither Gillan or Glover could have imagined at the time that not only would they wind up in a band that became one of the biggest in the world, but that they would both be performing and writing with Deep Purple more than fifty years later.

Brand's Hatch 18th June 1967

Ian Gillan at Luton Boys Club on 6th April 1968. Things could have been so different. With Deep Purple just a few miles away at Deeves Hall, South Mimms, Gillan could have been Purple's lead singer from the start and was suggested for the role by Nick Simper but turned down the fledgling band, believing that Episode Six would be more successful.

Keys Hall, Brentwood, 8th June 1968. When Episode Six's Sheila Carter-Dimmock took the lead vocal, Ian Gillan would sometimes take over on the organ. There would be no such chance to do that in Deep Purple!

Ian Gillan performing with Episode Six at the Silver End Hotel, Braintree, 18th August 1968. The hair was getting longer and by now the band had a new drummer Mick Underwood, formerly of The Outlaws alongside Blackmore. It was Underwood who instigated that Blackmore should check out the band's singer once again.

At Heathrow Airport, 3rd January 1969 having just returned from the first US tour. They had hit the ground running in the States but by the second tour in April '69 they were already finding gigs harder to come by Stateside and the band had been largely ignored in their homeland.

Deep Purple meets Episode Six. A very early publicity shot of the changed line-up taken in the summer of '69 at Hanwell Community Centre. It was during rehearsals at Hanwell that songs such as 'Speed King' and 'Child in Time' were created.

The band in rehearsal for Jon Lord's Concerto For Group & Orchestra. From day one Lord and Blackmore's love of orchestral music had been utilised in the band's songs. In fact both the classical and jazz elements in Purple's sound is often overlooked by the less initiated.

Jon Lord performing at the Pop and Blues Festival at the Grugahalle, Essen, 11th Oct 1969. It was gigs such as this that established MKII as a force to be reckoned with throughout Europe. For Lord, following the Concerto his writing input to the band took a back seat to those of Blackmore and new band members Gillan and Glover.

Blackmore and Gillan at De Lane Lea during the recording of the promotional film for 'Black Night'. The success of this non-album single track certainly helped increase sales of *In Rock*.

Ian Gillan photographed at the Royal Pavilion Gardens and on the beach in Brighton in May 1970. The photo session was to announce him as the voice of Jesus for the then, forthcoming rock opera Jesus Christ Superstar by the fledgling duo of Tim Rice and Andrew Lloyd-Webber. Rice had heard an early mix of 'Child in Time', which convinced him that Gillan would be perfect for the part.

Gillan recorded his parts in one afternoon at Olympic Studios in London. Whilst most of the other artists involved accepted a one-off session fee, Purple co-manager Tony Edwards took a chance on negotiating a royalty rate. It paid off as the following year the album was one of the biggest selling in the States.

With the collapse of the US record company in early 1970, the band concentrated on the European market and toured extensively both prior to and after the release of In Rock. This paid off with several radio and TV appearances such as this one at La Taverne de L'Olympia, Paris for French TV's "Pop Deux" on 8th October.

Arguably the two main factors in Deep Purple's success... as well as in it's ultimate break-up.

10
ROCK

The reviews for *Deep Purple In Rock* were overwhelmingly positive. *Disc* magazine said of it: 'At times, the album is 'Nice-ish', but, on the whole, a monster album and very exciting'[1]. For *Melody Maker*, it was a 'stunningly good' and 'magnificent' album that proved, among other things, that rock could be fresh and exciting, but also deep and meaningful — and that Blackmore was one hell of a guitarist[2]. *New Musical Express* minced no words in alluding to the central purpose of the album, which was, they wrote, to, 'put Deep Purple back on track after their brief flirtation with the classics'. The magazine went on to praise the way that, 'the guts and force of the group come to the boil and erupt in an ear-splitting frenzy. But quality is not sacrificed for volume'[3].

The single 'Black Night', backed by 'Speed King', was released on the same day as the album and was equally well received. Warners in the States released it in July with 'Into the Fire' as the B-side. *New Musical Express* argued that, 'To condense all [Deep Purple] have to offer into three minutes is asking a lot. But the boys have well nigh succeeded with this heavy rocker'[4].

Both records began a steady climb up the charts.

The more surprising of the two was the single. In the UK — finally! — it hit home, spending twenty-one weeks in the top 100, peaking at number two[5], although this should not be taken as definitive, since different charts existed at the time and some awarded it the top spot. It was not an instant smash, but one that took a while to find its place — most of that twenty-one week period was spent in a dogged and tenacious climb to the summit. Paice found the single's sales pattern puzzling: 'It's as confusing to us as to everybody else why the single was so slow selling. It was released at the same time as the album — that was at the beginning of June — and we gave it six weeks and thought it was finished. We went to America and thought it was another Purple miss in a long line of flops'[6]. As judgements go, this was a little harsh, since only 'Emmaretta' had been a total bomb in America — and there had been good reasons for that.

So successful was 'Black Night' that it propelled the band towards the first of their appearances on the British television show *Top of the Pops*: being accorded this honour was usually taken as a sign that a band had made it in the UK. Still rather sniffy about the whole culture around singles, it was seen as something of a necessary evil by most members of the band. Of the occasion, Glover said: 'You have to support the record, but we made our point by not plugging our guitars in. We didn't take it too seriously. We wanted to be ourselves and not pushed into any... slot'[7]. Gillan's take was: 'I know Ritchie hated 'TOTP' — it was associated with pop. Rock music had its own constituency, its own steering wheel. It was beyond the control of the establishment, and we saw TV as the enemy'[8].

Be that as it may, the publicity did not do the single any harm, since it also went to number two in Germany and number one in various other markets (Switzerland being a notable example). In the end, it sold just shy of an incredible two-and-a-half-million copies worldwide[9], making it, by far, the band's most successful single ever — eclipsing 'Hush'.

The album did even better. To date, it has sold nearly 6,000,000 copies worldwide, mostly in Europe[10]. It hit number one in Germany and Australia and number four in the UK[11], obliterating the band's previous best in their home market. Interestingly, it remains the lowest-selling of the four first-iteration Mark II albums in the USA, perhaps indicating how much work needed to be done to rebuild an American audience in the wake of Tetragrammaton's collapse. The album only managed to peak at a humble 143 on the Billboard 200 chart[12]. Still, it spent an impressive twenty-one weeks on the chart in the USA — and over a year on the charts in the UK[13].

Publicising the album through touring became the band's life for much of the next year. Of course, to some extent, the process had begun as early as the previous August with the introduction of 'Kneel and Pray' and 'Child in Time' into their live set. The 'Concerto' concert had been in the nature of a 'coming out ball' for the new material — as well as the band's approach to live performance during the early Mark II era. Another opportunity was an offer from the BBC in February to do an 'In Concert' appearance for broadcast on the radio.

Different from the BBC sessions of old, 'In Concert' involved a band being recorded at the BBC's Paris Theatre in London giving around an hour of their usual live set to a small, rather well behaved, audience. For Deep Purple, the invitation was very fortunate, since *In Rock* had not yet happened and, the 'Concerto' notwithstanding, they could have justifiably been considered a flash in the pan. Moreover, they were only drafted in at the last minute when Joe Cocker and The Grease Band cancelled unexpectedly.

The resulting recording was issued on vinyl (and, later,

CD) during the 1980s as a double album, the second disc comprising a 1972 'In Concert' date that concentrated on *Machine Head* material. Only the first disc concerns us here — and it is a fascinating listen.

The band's performance is, it should be said immediately, fantastic. A case can be made for 'In Concert' being one of Deep Purple's best live albums. It is exciting, innovative, cocksure — everything that the listener wants from a band of Mark II's sensibilities. The set list is short. A fairly straight 'Speed King' gets proceedings off to a fine start, before 'Child in Time' is given a run out. That's it for new material — reflecting where the band were with live performances at the time, as well, perhaps, as the current state of their songwriting.

Versions of 'Wring That Neck' and 'Mandrake Root' — clocking in at eighteen and seventeen minutes respectively — then follow[14]. As huge as these run times are, they are still brief compared to the lengths the two songs reached in more conventional concerts: presumably, the limitations of the BBC format encouraged the band to cut things down a bit. 'Mandrake Root's usual strobe-lit finale was, for example, severely truncated.

For 'In Concert', 'Wring That Neck' is elongated by solos from Lord and Blackmore that generally live up to their name in being minus any other band members (although Paice accompanies Lord for part of his, showing an almost supernatural ability to anticipate where the organist is going to go next).

Both solos are quite musical, using quotations from other works to add spice and dimension. It is perhaps telling that Lord alludes to the Norwegian composer Edvard Grieg, while Blackmore gives the listener a few bars of 'Jingle Bells'. Lord later gave his own take on such borrowings: 'We used to really enjoy those big long improvisations we did in those days, just seeing where we could take it and I would fling in a bit of [Antonín] Dvořák or something and [Blackmore] would smile and try and copy that and move it around somewhere"[15].

'Mandrake Root', by contrast, is something else entirely. The throbbing rhythm of the track continues throughout, the lead instrument solos that are laid over it entering the realms of the weird, the dissonant, the psychedelic and the arty. Lord's work, in particular, often resembles sound effects from a science fiction movie.

Both tracks could be described as more jazz than *rock 'n' roll*. 'Wring That Neck', in any case, is essentially a big band number: when it has been played on brass instruments — as at the 1999 'Concerto' revival — it has come across as something that Glenn Miller would have happily included in his oeuvre. Similarly, were the improvised sections of 'Mandrake Root' to be played on saxophones and trumpets, a sound not unlike the music of John Coltrane would be the result. All of this begs a question: were the early Mark II concerts heavy rock influenced by jazz or jazz played on heavy rock instruments?

It is important to stress that this applies only to live performances. There is little doubt that the recorded work, as can be heard on *In Rock* anyway, is heavy rock, but, as 'In Concert' demonstrates, Deep Purple on record and Deep Purple live were very different entities.

The choice of songs to be performed live brings this out very clearly. It is first worth noting the continuity with the past. Given the luxurious amount of space afforded 'Mandrake Root' and 'Wring That Neck', over half of any given gig consisted of Mark I material (on 'In Concert' the ratio is quite a bit more than half). Any notion that the recruitment of Gillan and Glover was regarded as an entirely fresh start is belied by this alone. Moreover, the 'Inglewood' recording from Mark I days indicates that the intention to use 'Mandrake Root' — at least — as a vehicle for extended soloing was already there, albeit to a more modest extent than would become the norm. That this situation continued for some time is proven by the release *Long Beach 1971*, which is a record of a gig that took place after the release of Deep Purple's next album, *Fireball*: 'Mandrake Root' is still the centre point.

The lengthy versions of songs — 'Mandrake Root' and 'Wring That Neck' most obviously, but also 'Child in Time' and others — did not come about by accident. A three-minute song does not expand to half an hour through sheer negligence. A decision must have been made to the effect that the songs would be used as frames for sounds that would exist nowhere else. This is the key point. Deep Purple's 1970 concerts were not merely about performing songs from the albums — they were about creating a music that was a thing in and of itself. So the bizarre noises of, for example, the live 'Mandrake Root' are not simply the solos from the albums taken to an extreme — they have no equivalent on the albums. The albums were made up of carefully constructed songs that would bear repeat listening. The concerts were a whole other art form: they may have taken their cues from the albums, but they moved off in free-form directions that were new, different and not capable of replication. Gillan noted this: 'Other bands used the word [improvisation] to disguise incompetence, but, in Purple's case, it was actually pretty good. There was an abstract approach to the music, very radical in those days. Actually, there's a particularly Purple approach to music... The structures, the flair, the flowing key changes, the riffs, the arrangements, the dynamics — tremendous dynamics. The texture of the music was light years ahead, or, at least, light years different, to what other bands were doing'[16]. It might even be suggested that Deep Purple were two separate bands — the album version and the live version. To experience either in isolation was to gain few clues about what the other might sound like.

Nowhere is this better to be seen than on the release known variously as *Scandinavian Nights*, *Live in Stockholm* or *Stockholm 1970*. Recorded on November 12th 1970, it is without a doubt one of the band's best live efforts. It also goes so far beyond anything recorded in the studio as to render any conversation about how the band translated their studio work into the live context moot.

The concert begins with a version of 'Speed King' that is over eleven minutes long. That leads on to 'Into the Fire' — a rare *In Rock* track to have a life on the stage. Then 'Child in Time' occupies the next nineteen minutes, before a thirty minute 'Wring That Neck', a 'Paint it, Black'-framed drum solo of twelve minutes and a 'Mandrake Root' that pulses away for another half an hour. The whole thing is brought to a close by 'Black Night', itself stretched out to over seven minutes.

Two hours, seven songs. That they were songs, though, was largely irrelevant. They were nothing more than hooks upon which to hang solos and improvisations. The important thing was the music. It all puts into perspective Gillan's often-made claim that Deep Purple are an instrumental band with vocal accompaniment: for over an hour of the Stockholm concert, his workload as vocalist consisted of precisely two verses of 'Mandrake Root'. Although no orchestra was present, it can be posited that the band had not entirely abandoned the forms and structures of the 'Concerto' — long passages of pure music, minimal inclusion of singing, an emphasis on the personalities and instruments of the main players. It may all be more Monk than Mozart, but the distance between the two is not quite as far as at first appears.

The year 1970 was essentially spent perfecting this set — and this approach. It worked, up to a point. America was temporarily on hold for the band — during dates over there in August, it became clear that not only did Warner not understand what the band were attempting to achieve with *In Rock*, but that the goodwill generated by 'Hush' had all but evaporated. The UK and Europe, though, were opening up in a big way.

One measure of this was increased interest from those hated TV people — although it seems that the band were prepared to be flexible on their anti-establishment principles for the sake of publicity. Not to be outdone by the BBC, Granada Television gave the band a short live slot on a programme called *Doing Their Thing*. The set was exactly the same as that for 'In Concert', although all of the songs were edited for broadcast — even 'Child in Time' suffered some surgery. On top of that, London Weekend Television broadcast a live version of 'Mandrake Root' as part of an event entitled *South Bank Summer*. Gillan was pleased with this one and it began to thaw him as far as TV was concerned (he had obviously forgotten that TV had been the life support machine for an ailing Episode Six during his tenure with that band). TV coverage in Europe also came the band's way — a live performance from Paris for French television being especially memorable[17].

The TV appearances were nuggets of glamour in what was otherwise a relentless slog around a multitude of small-to-medium-sized live venues situated in different parts of the UK — and the continent. Nowadays, a 'national' tour of the UK means dates at the four or five arenas capable of hosting large-scale events and which serve extensive hinterlands. A concert at Birmingham's NEC Arena, for example, is aimed at people from an area covering most of the west of England south of Manchester. That was not the case in the early 70s. A glance at Deep Purple's tour schedule for February 1970 reveals that they played the likes of Nottingham Boat Club, The King's Head

Blues Club, Romford, and St Mary's College, Twickenham.

Gigging took up much of the band's time, but the first half of the year was unusually busy in other areas. The sessions for *In Rock* were being fitted in between gigs, Paice and Blackmore were making their contributions to Derek Lawrence's 'Green Bullfrog' project, Gillan was off doing *Jesus Christ Superstar* and Lord was presumably writing the *Gemini Suite*. In the midst of it all, two notable incidents involving old acquaintances occurred – both of which had more-or-less serious longer term consequences.

The first centred on no less a figure than Mick Underwood. While recording the Quatermass album that would become as much his enduring legacy as anything else he ever did, he took advantage of a standing invitation to drop in on the *In Rock* sessions to have a listen and generally chew the fat with his old mates. While there, he played Blackmore a song on which he had been working - 'Black Sheep of the Family'. No one could possibly have known it then, but the seeds of Blackmore's eventual departure from the band — and, arguably, Deep Purple's complete dissolution — were sown that day[18].

The other twist in the plot brought back two figures from earlier in this story. In March, completely unexpectedly, Screaming Lord Sutch called Blackmore to invite him to jam with his band at the Country Club in Hampstead — the date of the proposed get-together being April 12th. He offered a hefty five-hundred-pound fee for the guitarist's participation. Unsurprisingly, Blackmore agreed and went along, unaware that another invitee was Nick Simper. Simper took part on the understanding that Albert Lee would be playing guitar — telling him that this would be the case was a straightforward piece of mendacity on Sutch's part. Gillan and Glover helped to bulk up the audience. Simper was, not unnaturally, mortified, but did the gig anyway. He later said that, '[Blackmore] was on one side and I was on the other and that was it. We didn't speak"[19].

Even so, the occasion proved to be the beginning of a thaw in relations. The release of Warhorse's self-titled debut album was Blackmore's excuse to get in touch with the former Purple bassist to offer congratulations. From there, something like a friendship developed. These events found their echo in later years when Blackmore invited Glover — whose removal from Deep Purple was also Blackmore's initiative — to join Rainbow. It seemed that, for all his moodiness, the 'man in black' was not without a more sentimental side.

For the band as a whole, the hard work was beginning to pay off. Their popularity was rising, although it would still be some time before it peaked. In August, they played the Plumpton Jazz and Blues Festival — the same event at which they had received an, at best, lukewarm response two years earlier. This time, the crowd went wild, partly as a result of Blackmore having Ian Hansford set fire to his amps in order to upstage the de facto headliners, Yes. Unfortunately, the flames took hold and set light to the stage's backdrop. Chaos was the predictable result, although Blackmore, ever the showman, took advantage of it to throw around his guitar and generally behave in a way that could best be described as 'unrestrained'. With typical insouciance, his only comment was: 'Actually, we meant to set the whole stage alight'[20].

At other gigs, something akin to a type of 'Purplemania' was emerging. While it lacked the political and social change elements of Beatlemania, it was manifested at gigs in much the same way: girls – often screaming - threw themselves at the band members, particularly Gillan. Rowdiness, occasionally bordering on hooliganism and violence, infected crowds. This happened to such an extent that Gillan was actually forced to address the issue in an interview given in December, during dates in Germany. Having praised the 'beautiful' atmosphere at gigs, he went on to say that there were a lot of people 'outside' venues who thought that the music ought to be free and who caused trouble as a result. He accused them of 'smashing windows' and 'fighting'[21].

One thing for sure was that Deep Purple were not an underground band anymore. They had genuine fans. They had conquered the mainstream and annexed it for hard rock.

Little time was given to enjoying any of this, or the success of *In Rock*, which, as magnificent a product as it was, had not furnished the band with much in the way of live material — beyond the tracks that had pre-dated it by several months. In truth, Mark II were touring a set that largely consisted of Mark I songs and a cover ('Paint it Black'). It may have been felt that more new material was needed urgently, so attention turned to the next album. Although the intention was to record it in one quick blast, it ended up being laid down in much the same way as its illustrious predecessor — ground out between gigs over an extended period.

The first session took place in September. If the expectation was that it would produce another fuzzbox classic to rank with 'Speed King' or 'Hard Lovin' Man', it was soon dashed. Instead, all that appeared was a mainly acoustic country-style song, 'Anyone's Daughter'. Memorable mainly for Gillan's witty story-telling lyrics, it is entertaining enough, but so far away from anything on *In Rock* as to sound like the work of an entirely different band.

Thanks to a myriad of other commitments, no further work was carried out on what would become *Fireball* until December. Indeed, that is how Deep Purple finished 1970 and the period covered by this book — much as they had started it, at a country house rehearsing songs for a new album. This time, the setting was Welcombe Manor in Devon.

What was accomplished took the band down a different road from that taken on *In Rock*. The December sessions produced the song that would become the next single, 'Strange Kind of Woman', which would be enough of a hit to get the band on to *Top of the Pops* for a second time (clearly, no-one associated with that show bothered to read the lyrics, which are blatantly about a prostitute called Nancy — indeed, the song's working title was 'Prostitute').

The only other output from Welcombe was 'Freedom', which is the one song from this period that would have sounded at home on *In Rock*. It was rejected. Its first release was on the 1985 *Anthology* compilation.

When it eventually appeared, *Fireball* had little in common with *In Rock*. Although the fuzzbox was still a factor, it was heavily toned down. The album's overall feel was prog, bordering, at times, on funk. Experiments with song structure were very much to the fore. The title track was a stormer, however, being about as close to thrash metal as Deep Purple have ever got.

As a way to encapsulate the argument followed here, this is as good a place to end as any. It illustrates perfectly the sense of continuity in the Deep Purple story as well as the way in which the music constantly evolved. *Fireball* – released in 1971 - would prove to be another big seller, as well as a high water mark of Deep Purple creativity. But, like its predecessors, it did not appear ex nihilo. The roots were there. The roots were always there.

And so we come back to hindsight. With hindsight, we can see that Gillan and Glover joining the band was a step change that ushered in a new age — Mark II — which produced in *In Rock* something completely different from anything that had gone before. But that is to look at events through a lens that was not available at the time. The album was unlike the band's previous output, for sure, but it was not without antecedents — both from within the band and from other sources. Its seeds had been sown several years earlier during the formative musical lives of those who played upon it. More immediately, it was a self-conscious reaction to Deep Purple's increasingly close association with orchestras, string quartets and all things prog. Even then, the rejection was not total and *In Rock* lived quite comfortably alongside those prog elements for some time in live settings; the dropping of Mark I material from the band's set happened at much the same moment that *In Rock* itself was stressed less than the all-powerful juggernaut that was *Machine Head* — which became the ore from which live playlists were smelted.

Above all, *In Rock* owed its existence to the increasing dominance of the fuzzbox in rock music. Deep Purple had used it before, although it had tended to occupy a less exalted place than its cousin, the wah-wah pedal. But it was not to be denied. As it began to define the sounds of the Led Zeppelins, The Rolling Stoneses and, over all, that high priest of the fuzzbox, Jimi Hendrix, it was inevitable that a band of Deep Purple's ambitions would, at some point, adopt it. Perhaps the most surprising aspect of *In Rock* is just how much of a full-blooded adoption it would be — so complete that the band themselves would never go to that place again.

Sculpting In Rock

11
TODAY

We have considered the archaeology of *In Rock*, but what of its legacy? How did it fit into the ongoing history of Deep Purple and, perhaps, rock music in general?

The answer to the first of these questions can relatively easily be given: as we have argued, it was never repeated. This is not necessarily a bad thing.

Fireball was every bit as experimental as its predecessor. Eschewing the full-on fuzzbox attack of *In Rock*, it adopted a range of different styles. Funk, prog and, yes, classical appeared in a set that was as surprising in its own way as anything the band had ever done. Indeed, there is a case for *Concerto for Group and Orchestra*, *In Rock* and *Fireball* being Deep Purple's true creative peak, their ultimate trilogy of greatness.

Such a view is controversial because next came *Machine Head*, but was the creative well already running dry by then? Discuss. Certainly, by the time of *Who Do We Think We Are*, their fourth album together, Mark II were a spent force and it is not entirely surprising that Blackmore's restlessness saw in Gillan's resignation an opportunity to eject Glover and take a different direction.

Recruiting David Coverdale on vocals and Glenn Hughes on bass and vocals, the band became bluesier and funkier — not that this was too much in evidence on the first Mark III release, *Burn*, which is another outstanding example of Deep Purple artistry. As much of a watershed in its own way as *In Rock*, it is a stunning piece of work that ushered in what should have been a brilliant new era for the band. Sadly, the follow-up to *Burn*, *Stormbringer*, was another mish-mash of genres, but it was no *Fireball*. While it is hard to agree with Blackmore — who called it 'crap' — its odd mixture of heavy rock and unadorned funk (and even soul) makes for a strange listen and one that does not come close to the coherence and inventiveness of *Burn*. For Blackmore, it was the end and he left to form Rainbow.

The others carried on, recruiting American wunderkind Tommy Bolin, to form Mark IV. One album resulted, *Come Taste the Band*. Often dismissed as 'not a Deep Purple album'[1], it is, in fact, a classic — and arguably the closest the band ever got to recreating the sound of *In Rock*. Powerful, intense and incorporating other styles without — as on *Stormbringer* — surrendering to them, it is a superb rock album with few, if any, low points.

It was, however, another false dawn and the band split for what was, in hindsight, an eight year hiatus. Reforming in 1984 with the Mark II line-up, fans salivated at the possibility of what was — by common consent — the best iteration of Deep Purple coming back to bless the world with its music. Things did not turn out quite that way. The first album, *Perfect Strangers*, was good, although not the hoped-for masterwork. It did attempt to invoke the spirit of *In Rock* on tracks like 'Under the Gun' and 'Mean Streak', but these were unusual — much of the album sounded suspiciously like the music that Blackmore had been making with Rainbow. Its successor, *The House of Blue Light*, flattered to deceive with a title taken from the lyrics of 'Speed King'. In actuality, it was a piece of late-

'80s MOR that sounded nothing like Deep Purple at their most characteristic[2].

From there, personnel turmoil led to the sacking of Gillan and the ex-Rainbow singer Joe Lynn Turner-fronted, *Slaves and Masters* album, before the Mark II line-up reconvened for one last time to produce *The Battle Rages On...* — probably the most disappointing album that the band have ever made. Released to coincide with their twenty-fifth anniversary, a second *In Rock* might have been expected. Or, if not that, at least something that expressed the grandeur and creativity of the band at their best, something epic, symphonic, filled with soon-to-be classics. No such luck. *The Battle Rages On...* sounds like a bunch of out-takes from the Rainbow album, *Long Live Rock 'n' Roll*. Guitar and riff-led, with clichéd song titles, tired lyrics and an almost complete absence of Jon Lord, it is a poor way to mark an important moment in the band's history.

It also begs an important question: just how good were Mark II, really? For all the veneration that they receive, it should not be forgotten that two of their albums are among the worst that the band have produced (*The House of Blue Light* and *The Battle Rages On...*), another two are no better than okay (*Who Do We Think We Are* and *Perfect Strangers*) and only three studio albums and two live albums actually stand up as excellent (the 'trilogy' discussed above plus *Machine Head* and *Made in Japan*). One of these does not include new material. Of course, many bands would love to have even this much greatness in their catalogue, but it does illustrate the truth that Deep Purple's most fertile period was a relatively brief three-year blast that even the men responsible for it could not repeat.

The Battle Rages On... was the end of the road (literally) for Blackmore, who quit for a second time mid-tour, leaving the others to soldier on, firstly with Joe Satriani, and then Steve Morse. The first album of the 'Morse era' was an experimental belter in *Purpendicular*. Another mix of styles, the main emotion that hit most fans upon hearing it for the first time was relief — the boys had still got it! Phew! But, again, the renaissance was short-lived.

The next release, *Abandon* was not bad — it was probably the heaviest the band had been since *In Rock*, a track from which it featured as a remake. It was, though, Lord's last outing with the band: he left in 2002 to pursue a career as a classical composer. The equally talented Don Airey was drafted in as a replacement and the battle raged on...

Unfortunately, the next album, *Bananas* — the first to not feature Lord — was, to the ears of many, the band's creative nadir, despite, bafflingly, containing Gillan's favourite Deep Purple song (the fan non-favourite, 'Razzle Dazzle').

After a three year wait, *Rapture of the Deep* came out and it was not much of an improvement. At this point, Deep Purple were still alive, but largely as a nostalgia act. It seemed that their best days as songwriters were long behind them. For a while, 'Rapture' had 'last album' written all over it, years passing with no announcements about upcoming releases. It would have been the weakest of whimpers upon which to end...

It proved not to be so, because the legendary rock producer Bob Ezrin entered the picture to take matters in hand. He was the perfect collaborator, leading on three unexpectedly good albums in quick succession, 2013's *Now What!?*, *Infinite* from 2017 and, in 2020, *Whoosh!* This 'Time Trilogy', as it has been informally dubbed, represents the band's most sustained run of creativity since the 'Concerto' to *Fireball* sequence.

It also features a new lyrical seriousness on the part of the band (*Whoosh!*, despite its title, was trailed as being about 'putting the 'deep' back into 'Deep Purple"). Every album since the 1984 reformation had featured at least one song that meant absolutely nothing — 'A Gypsy's Kiss' on *Perfect Strangers*, for example, or the Molesworth-inspired 'Any Fule Kno That' on *Abandon* — but these were noticeably less in evidence on the Ezrin-produced albums. In their place were political statements and story-telling: the middle album of the three, *Infinite*, is basically an anthology of unlikely, but, allegedly, true, tales, with Gillan in his past lives as the central character.

Another trend within the 'trilogy' is that of a return to the band's Mark I roots. More prog than hard rock, many of the tracks are keyboard-led - reflecting the extent to which Airey's ideas influence the sound. There are also cover versions and instrumental lead-ins to songs not unlike the 'preludes' that appear on the first three albums[3]. One track on *Now What!?* ('Hell to Pay') has an instrumental section reminiscent of 'Mandrake Root', while *Whoosh!* includes a remake of 'And the Address'. There are even strings here and there. This should not be taken too far — the Time Trilogy does not sound too much like the Mark I albums, but it is in the same tradition; it can be imagined that this is where the band would have gone sooner had *In Rock* not happened.

The most recent — as of writing — Deep Purple release is even more of a deep dive into their past. *Turning to Crime* is a full-on covers album, the band's most sustained collection of covers since *The Book of Taliesyn*. Of most interest, however, is the source of the songs chosen. Only one track ('Dixie Chicken') comes from a date after 1970 — and that is early 70s. Most are from the 1960s, from the time when the members of Deep Purple were starting out, getting their first taste of rock star life, or just dreaming of what might be. If the Time Trilogy is a nostalgic trip back to the good old days, then *Turning to Crime* is a journey to the days before the good old days.

What this brief historical sketch should emphasise is that *In Rock*, for all of its innovation, exists as part of a continuum. It did not come from nowhere — we have already established that — but it was also only partly a template for what happened later. The glory of Deep Purple is their variety. Yes, they can play dirty, grungy fuzzbox-driven music with the best of them, but they can also sit alongside an orchestra. *In Rock* must be seen as a crowning achievement, for sure, but it is not the band's only achievement.

So, what about the fans? What about me? What does the album mean to this middle-aged, jaded-by-experience, man today?

Perhaps the best way to answer that would be to go back a decade or so to a place that I have spent much of my time with Deep Purple, the NEC Arena in Birmingham. As I had been many times before, I was in the audience one night, flanked by other lone men, belying their ages with leather jackets and heavy rock themed t-shirts. The band was engaged in what they called their 'orchestra tour'. Essentially, this meant performing a fairly standard gig, but, as the title suggests, with the addition of an orchestra to provide backing, dimension and tone. So no sections from the 'Concerto', or any of Jon Lord's other experiments were played — simply the songs, rounded out with strings, brass and percussion. For much of the band's catalogue, this was a superb idea, given how much of it already has a classical basis. The orchestra-backed version of the song 'Perfect Strangers', for example, is so good that it really should be viewed as definitive.

Some parts of *In Rock* would be plausible candidates for this treatment. 'Child in Time' with an orchestral boost is a mouth-watering prospect: it would surely be a glorious reinvention of a song that has not been performed live by the band for what is now decades. That is not, however, the route down which they decided to go. The *In Rock* song that they chose was 'Hard Lovin' Man'.

Now, of all the tracks on the album — heck, of all Deep Purple tracks — this would have struck me as the least suitable for inclusion in the set of such a gig. With its super heavy staccato riff, insane keyboards and general air of barely-controlled anarchy, it must surely have nothing to offer the discipline and control of an orchestra — must it?

At the appropriate point in the concert, the riff kicked in. I half expected this to be the moment that the orchestra would take a break to let the band do their stuff alone for a few minutes. But, no! Violins were placed under chins, trumpets raised to lips, timpani readied and then — the orchestra started to play the riff. The string section worked overtime jabbing at the air with their bows, mirroring the intensity of the band. The brass provided sharp stabs during the chorus flourishes. The percussion added deep pounding rumbles to everything. It was glorious. Not only could the song survive the transition to this new performance style, it thrived. The orchestra found depths and subtleties in the music of which even the band must not, up to that point, have been aware.

That night, that black night, it became blindingly obvious to me that the durability of *In Rock* comes not from mere fan loyalty, or the support of a pliant music press, but the vital, living nature of the music itself. 'Hard Lovin' Man' was revealed to be not just a proto-thrash metal anthem, but a resilient and adaptable piece of art, one with enough depth to make it a natural pairing with that highest expression of high culture, orchestral music.

In Rock, then, may not be perfect in every way — it is sometimes incoherently loud and, lyrically, is often wilfully obscure — but it might just be perfect in form. From its opening moment of mayhem to its closing moment of mayhem, it has a drive and purpose that characterises all of the greatest works of art. It is the product of creators determined to pursue a particular vision with little regard for how it would be received. In this respect (if, to be fair, in few others), it can be ranked with *The Waste Land*, *Apocalypse Now* and many another artistic landmark. It is particularly noteworthy that this is achieved with the simplest of palettes: vocals, guitar, organ, bass, drums. The pianos, Moog synthesisers and harmonised backing vocals of later releases are entirely absent.

Compare it to other great rock albums. To take one, *Led Zeppelin 4* (or whatever it is called) is without doubt a great album. It has absolutely nothing to prove; its place in cultural history is assured. But it cannot be said to have a strong cohesive structure. Its songs range over various styles, from hard rock, to straight up rock 'n' roll, to folk, to acoustic pop songs. All are excellent on their own terms, but the album as a whole is more an anthology than a single artistic statement.

Not so *In Rock*: its songs are all of a piece, without sounding the same. They take the listener on a journey that is wide and broad in scope, but all within a single, uncompromising vision. They surprise, delight, shock at times and, yes, it must be said, exhaust, but they never, ever, bore.

For me, that Fame cassette has long since disappeared and, anyway, even if I still had it, I no longer possess anything to play it on. It would perhaps have some nostalgia value... That aside, I have a couple of CDs of the album, both of the twenty-fifth anniversary edition, nestling on my (appallingly disorganised) shelves at home somewhere. Even they, now, are more-or-less unplayable, the Mac computer that was the last redoubt of the CD-compatible disk drive in my house having similarly succumbed to time. Instead, I have a download on my phone and on my iPad. Again, this is of the deluxe remastered version of the album. It can truthfully be said that I never leave home without my copy of *Deep Purple In Rock*.

A good question is why we — and by this I do mean 'we', dear reader — listen to heavy music at all — what does it do for us? The fuzzbox does not, after all, create particularly pretty noises. As we have seen, heavy rock fans are among the more gentle and non-threatening of people: does that have something to do with the music? Some studies have suggested not[4].

In one lab test, mice who had been played a steady stream of Mozart were peaceable and co-operative, whereas those who had been given a relentless diet of heavy metal ended up killing each other. Happily, orgies of communal murder are, in my experience, rare at rock gigs. This is because humans are not mice and we are hard-wired with an ethical awareness that precludes allowing ourselves to reach such level of violence — in most cases. Heavy music has been found to be a means by which anger can be processed constructively[5]. In other words, it calms a person down (although this effect is more noticeable in fans than non-fans).

It also helps people who have suffered a trauma. To some extent, this is to do with the lyrical content of many heavy rock songs — the sense of shared experience is a point of connection between a traumatised individual and a community of listeners who, perhaps, are going through the same or similar. In effect, then, heavy rock is a giant virtual mutual support group. For me, the music of Deep Purple as a whole, but *In Rock*, in particular, serves to endow me with that — admittedly abstract — feeling of community and group membership.

Even so, I do not listen to the album all the time. Or all that often, if I am being absolutely honest. In line with the research referenced above, it serves a turn when I am feeling down, or in need of a little energising, but generally it just sits there with the patience of an artefact that has already been with us for fifty plus years and is likely to be with us for a long time to come. I would not be without it, but it does not need to be listened to with religious regularity. It does its job of linking me to the person I once was and the person that that person has become — with Deep Purple as a defining influence.

If, therefore, I were one of those YouTubers giving my ranking of Deep Purple's studio albums (including live albums would complicate matters by bringing in the 'Concerto', 'In Concert' and 'Stockholm' - among others), what would be my top five? Would I go with the old consensus and place *Machine Head* at the apex? Would it be runner-up, if not? Actually, for me, it would only come in at number four.

In fifth place, I would put *Come Taste the Band*, which has demonstrated its staying power and sounds far fresher than many more recent releases, its venerability notwithstanding. In fourth, *Machine Head*. It's a monumental album, for sure, but, to me, it increasingly sounds like a retreat to formula and the moment at which musical experiments largely ended.

My top three would begin with *Fireball*. What can I say? It is not the heaviest album going and, stylistically, it is a bit all over the place — Blackmore, unfairly said of it, 'I just don't see anything on *Fireball* that's worth even thinking about; that's a personal thing. I would never play it'[6]. I would have to agree that it is a personal thing: as far as I am concerned, *Fireball* is inventive, creative and entertaining, so what is not to love about it?

First among the losers would be *Burn*. It might surprise some that an album that does not feature Gillan and Glover is so high up the list, but it is so for both personal and artistic reasons. It was the first Deep Purple album that I bought as an eager fourteen-year-old and is, by any reckoning, an epic rock achievement. From its immense title track onwards, it is a cornucopia of musical brilliance, embracing all kinds of genres and styles, but without losing its own distinct identity.

That only leaves the top spot, my favourite Deep Purple studio album. Well, what do you think it is? There can be only one, the ultimate album by the band, perhaps the ultimate hard rock album full stop. The album that the fuzzbox was invented for. On those occasions when I do listen to it, what can I do but take the full force of its blast, close my eyes and wait for the ricochet?

Sculpting In Rock

Notes and References

1   Boxes

1. Noke-Edwards, L. (2020). Breaking Down the Science and History Behind Your Favourite Fuzz Tones. Mixdown Mag, https://mixdownmag.com.au/features/what-the-fuzz-breaking-down-the-science-behind-your-favourite-fuzzy-tones/ [accessed Saturday 15th January 2022]

2. Distortion was first introduced as early as the 1940s by guitarists looking for a 'dirtier sound' for blues-based music. At that stage, however, it was not so much a deliberate artificial effect as a natural consequence of turning amps up to their highest level (https://www.openculture.com/2018/09/brief-history-guitar-distortion-early-experiments-happy-accidents-classic-effects-pedals.html)

3. https://www.wideopencountry.com/how-marty-robbins-accidentally-pioneered-guitar-fuzz-effects/ [accessed Friday 14th January 2022]

4. Dr No's Little History Lesson about Guitar Effects, https://shop.drno-effects.com/drnos-little-history-lesson-about-guitar-effects/ [accessed Friday January 14th 2022]

5. Weir, W. (2011). 50 Years of Making Fuzz, the sound that Defines Rock 'n' Roll. The Atlantic, March 3.

6. Weinstein, D. (2014). Just So Stories: How Heavy Metal Got Its Name — A Cautionary Tale. Rock Music Studies, 1(1).

7. Jon Lord interview with Jerry Bloom, 21st November 2007.

8. Crowe, C. (1973). Deep Purple: Self-Evaluation Time Again. *Rolling Stone*, June 21st 1973.

2 Tapes

1. Robinson, S. (1995). *Deep Purple In Rock Anniversary Edition*, CD Booklet.

2. Ritchie Blackmore interview with *Disc and Music Echo*, June 6th 1970.

3. McIver, J. (2020). How Deep Purple's Classic In Rock Was Made. *Classic Rock*, https://www.loudersound.com/features/deep-purple-the-making-of-in-rock [accessed Saturday 15th January 2022].

4. Jon Lord interview on Igor's Deep Purple Universe, 28th May 2009 https://youtu.be/umVoclBiGwY [accessed Sunday 16th January 2022].

5. Smith, R. (2012). Jon Lord: Deep Purple's Lord of the Amps. *The Globe and Mail*, July 18th 2012.

6. Clarke, L. (1986). Leslie: Pipe Voice of the Electric Organ. Theatre Organ, May-June, 12-14.

7. Jon Lord Interview November 2010. *Darker Than Blue*, https://darkerthanblue.wordpress.com/interviews/jon-lord-interview-november-2010/ [accessed Sunday 16th January 2022].

8. Jon Lord Interview. Deep Purple Official, https://youtu.be/0yNoMh2w1NM [accessed Monday 17th January 2022].

9. Robinson, S. (2014). *Wait for the Ricochet: The Story of Deep Purple in Rock*. Easy on the Eye Books.

10. *Stargazer* magazine (2020). Legendary producer Martin Birch (1948-2020) remembered. https://stargazed.net/fallen-heroes/legendary-producer-martin-birch-1948-2020-remembered/ [accessed Sunday 16th January 2022].

11. *Darker Than Blue*, https://darkerthanblue.wordpress.com/another-service-from-darker-than-blue-magazine/recording-made-in-japan/ [accessed Thursday 20th January 2022].

12. Deep Purple — loud and proud. *Melody Maker*, August 15th 1970.

13. Interview with Ritchie Blackmore. https://youtu.be/pLgF7BDch4M [accessed Monday 17th January 2022].

14. Caramba! Wordography http://www.gillan.com/wordography-65.html [accessed Monday 17th January 2022].

15. Top 2000 a gogo: Deep Purple — Child in Time. The Story Behind the Song. https://youtu.be/OkveukuxQ3Y [accessed Tuesday 18th January 2022].

16. Top 2000 a gogo: Deep Purple — Child in Time. The Story Behind the Song. https://youtu.be/OkveukuxQ3Y [accessed Tuesday 18th January 2022].

17. It is surprising how popular 'Wring That Neck' seems to have been as a source for other musicians. Ex-Purple bassist Nick Simper's post-Purple band Warhorse, for example, released a song entitled 'Ritual', which is little more than 'Wring That Neck' with vocals. It is, perhaps, a testament to the musical power of the track.

18. Caramba! Wordogrraphy https://www.gillan.com/wordography-16.html [accessed Tuesday 18th January 2022].

19. *Melody Maker*, August 1970.

20. Top 2000 a gogo: Deep Purple — Child in Time. The Story Behind the Song. https://youtu.be/OkveukuxQ3Y [accessed Tuesday 18th January 2022].

21. Jon Lord interview 28th May 2009. https://youtu.be/umVoclBiGwY [accessed Wednesday 19th January 2022].

22. Robinson, S. (2014). *Wait for the Ricochet: The Story of Deep Purple in Rock*. Easy on the Eye Books.

23. Gillan, I. (2016). *Ian Gillan: The Autobiography of Deep Purple's Lead Singer*. Music Press.

24. Bennet, S. (2016). Behind the magical mystery door: history, mythology and the aura of Abbey Road Studios. Popular Music, 35(3), 396-417.

25. Bienstock, R. (2021). The Unstoppable Rise of Ritchie Blackmore and the Making of *Deep Purple in Rock*'. *Guitar Player*, https://www.guitarplayer.com/players/the-unstoppable-rise-of-ritchie-blackmore-and-the-making-of-deep-purple-in-rock [accessed Saturday 22nd January 2022].

26. Robinson, S. (1995). *Deep Purple In Rock Anniversary Edition*, CD Booklet.

27. Bloom, J. (2011). *Deep Purple Uncensored On The Record*. Coda Books Ltd.

28. Ibid.

29. Ritchie Blackmore on his Inspiration and Thievery. Ritchie Blackmore Channel https://youtu.be/l22yOjWthGI [accessed Saturday 22nd January 2022].

30. Ritchie Blackmore Interview with Neil Jeffries, September 9th 1995.

31. Deep Purple — Late Keyboard Legend Jon Lord Talks About 'Black Night' Hit: Rare Video. Brave Words, https://bravewords.com/news/deep-purple-late-keyboard-legend-jon-lord-talks-about-black-night-hit-rare-video [accessed Tuesday 29th March 2022].

32. The Making of Black Night. *Rumba Magazine*, 1993.

33. Deep Purple — Late Keyboard Legend Jon Lord Talks About 'Black Night' Hit: Rare Video. Brave Words, https://bravewords.com/news/deep-purple-late-keyboard-legend-jon-lord-talks-about-black-night-hit-rare-video [accessed Wednesday 23rd March 2022].

34. *Melody Maker*, 1969.

35. *New Musical Express*, August 2nd 1969.

36. Ibid.

37. Robinson, S. (1995). *Deep Purple In Rock Anniversary Edition*, CD Booklet.

38. *Melody Maker*, August 2nd 1969.

39. The first Deep Purple album that does not, in some way, represent the

band's members on the cover is 1975's *Stormbringer*: this features a moody picture of a tornado, which appears to have opened a rift in the sky through which a winged horse (the 'stormbringer' perhaps — it is not made very clear in the title song's lyrics what a 'stormbringer' actually is). Even the cover of the second album — *The Book of Taliesyn* — includes ink drawings of minstrels that are presumably intended to represent the band's members. Since the band re-formed in 1984, only the sleeve to their 2021 covers album *Turning to Crime* has included pictures of the band. In many ways, this is a better gauge of changing tastes than the music itself.

40. ST33 https://st33.wordpress.com/sleeve-artists-designers/deep-purple-in-rock/ [accessed Saturday 22nd January 2022].

3.   Roots

1. Lawrence, D. I've been working like a dog: Revisiting a 1960s study of the working class. University of Cambridge Research, https://www.cam.ac.uk/research/news/ive-been-working-like-a-dog-revisiting-a-1960s-study-of-the-working-class [accessed Sunday 23rd January 2022].
2. His family moved to Heston in Middlesex when he was two years old. Any putative meeting between himself and John Cleese would, then, have been unwitting on his part.
3. Interview inserts to the live video release *Come Hell or High Water* (1994).
4. Me and My Music. *Disc and Music Echo*, September 19th 1970.
5. Bloom, J. (2015). *The Road of Golden Dust: The Deep Purple Story 1968-1976*. Wymer Publishing.
6. Me and My Music. *Disc and Music Echo*, September 19th 1970.
7. Bloom, J. (2011). *Deep Purple Uncensored On The Record*. Coda Books Ltd.
8. Jon Lord about composing, his music career and the developments in the music industry. https://www.xecutives.net/jon-lord-about-composing-his-music-career-and-the-developments-in-the-music-industry/ [accessed Tuesday 25th January 2022].
9. Ibid.
10. Bloom, J. (2015). *The Road of Golden Dust: The Deep Purple Story 1968-1976*. Wymer Publishing.
11. Ibid.
12. Wikimetal, https://www.wikimetal.com.br/interview-with-ian-gillan/ [accessed Thursday 27th January 2022].
13. Bloom, J. (2011). *Deep Purple Uncensored On The Record*. Coda Books Ltd.
14. Gillan, I. (2016). *Ian Gillan: The Autobiography of Deep Purple's Lead Singer*. Music Press.
15. *Roger Glover: Made in Wales*. ITV Wales Documentary.
16. Bloom, J. (2011). *Deep Purple Uncensored On The Record*. Coda Books Ltd.
17. Bloom, J. (2006). *Black Knight: Ritchie Blackmore*. Omnibus Press. Joe Meek was an eccentric character, to say the least. His recording methods were outwardly chaotic, although everything was well-catalogued in his head. Because he had a habit of recording musicians and then using their work on different releases, it is impossible to say exactly which tracks featured the young Blackmore. Unfortunately, any hope of tapping the source and solving the mystery was quashed on February 3rd 1967, when Meek, suffering from depression, took a shotgun that he had borrowed from Heinz Burt and used it to kill first his landlady, Violet Shenton, and then himself.

18   Crowe, C. (1975). Ritchie Blackmore — Shallow Purple. *Rolling Stone*, no. 184.

19.   Ibid.

20.   Ian Paice Drumtribe https://youtu.be/727rvc8J5Vc [accessed Saturday 29th January 2022].

21.   Ibid

22.   Nick Simper Interview with *Darker Than Blue* 1983 https://www.nicksimper.net/darker-blue-interview/ [accessed Monday 7th February 2022].

23.   Green, R. (1971). Jon Lord — refugee from the flowerpot men. *New Musical Express*, March 13th 1971.

24.   Gillan, I. (2016). *Ian Gillan: The Autobiography of Deep Purple's Lead Singer*. Music Press.

25.   Episode Six family tree. Deep Purple.net http://www.deep-purple.net/tree/episode-six/episode-six-1.html [accessed Sunday 30th January 2022].

26.   Musicguy247, Interview with Mick Underwood https://musicguy247.typepad.com/my-blog/2018/01/mick-underwood-quatermass-ian-gillan-ritchie-blackmore-the-outlaws-jet-harris-drums-paul-rodgers-episode-six-glory-road-strap.html [accessed Monday 31st January 2022].

27.   Ibid

28.   The Deep Purple Podcast Episode 6 — Episode Six https://deeppurplepodcast.com/2019/06/03/episode-6-episode-six/ [accessed Wednesday 2nd February 2022].

29.   Ritchie Blackmore Interview with Neil Jeffries, September 9th 1995.

30.   Sweeting, A. (2005). Chris Curtis. *The Guardian* https://www.theguardian.com/news/2005/mar/03/guardianobituaries.artsobituaries [accessed Thursday 3rd February 2022).

31.   Leigh, S. (1997). Interview with Chris Curtis. *Record Collector*.

32.   Ibid

33.   Ibid

4. Rehearsals

1. Perrone, P. (2010). Tony Edwards: Entrepreneur who managed Deep Purple, Toyah Wilcox and Johnny Clegg. The Independent, November 22nd 2010.

2. Arguably, the ways in which the first three 'marks' of Deep Purple came about indicate that the 'roundabout' concept never really went away. Mark I gave way to Mark II when the singer and bass guitarist were replaced at the same time. Likewise, a change of singer and bassist resulted in Mark III. Blackmore, Lord and Paice remained at the core throughout. Only when Blackmore left the band in 1975, thus instituting Mark IV, could it be said that the roundabout idea truly died.

3. *Darker Than Blue* https://darkerthanblue.wordpress.com/obituaries/tony-edwards/ [accessed Friday 4th February 2022].

4. Speaking years after the fact, Derek Lawrence painted a picture of how the arrangement worked, claiming, not unfairly, that he did much to secure the band some very favourable deals as they were setting out. He stated that Coletta suffered from a certain amount of hubris that drove him to believe that 'he suddenly knew it all'; 'He would have an opinion — it was probably never right — but he would have his own opinion'. Lawrence characterised Edwards as a business man, rather than a music man, who would 'say 'that's great' if he heard someone say 'that's great' before him'. https://youtu.be/p2UNVsX60LI

5. Bloom, J. (2011). *Deep Purple Uncensored On The Record*. Coda Books Ltd.

6. Leigh, S. (1997). Interview with Chris Curtis. *Record Collector*.

7. Ritchie Blackmore Interview with Neil Jeffries, September 9th 1995.

8. Jon Lord interviewed for the *BBC Rock Family Trees* documentary on Deep Purple.

9. Ritchie Blackmore Interview with Neil Jeffries, September 9th 1995.

10. Leigh, S. (1997). Interview with Chris Curtis. *Record Collector*.

11. Tyler, K. On the Roundabout with Deep Purple. Deep Purple Appreciation Society http://www.deep-purple.net/archive/68-76history/roundabout.htm [accessed Monday 7th February 2022].

12. Green, R. (1971). Jon Lord — refugee from the flowerpot men. *New Musical Express*, March 13th 1971.

13. Nick Simper Interview with *Darker Than Blue* 1983 https://www.nicksimper.net/darker-blue-interview/ [accessed Monday 7th February 2022].

14. Tyler, K. On the Roundabout with Deep Purple. Deep Purple Appreciation Society http://www.deep-purple.net/archive/68-76history/roundabout.htm [accessed Monday 7th February 2022].

15. Ibid

16. Nick Simper Interview with *Darker Than Blue* 1983 https://www.nicksimper.net/darker-blue-interview/ [accessed Tuesday 8th February 2022].

17. If photographs are to be believed, Deeves Hall is a rather lovely place,

comprising a large white manor-style house, a barn and a good quantity of carefully landscaped gardens. The fifty-pounds-a-month rent that the management supposedly paid was a lot of money back then, but it bought a lot of good vibe-laden real estate.

18. Nick Simper Interview with *Darker Than Blue* 1983 https://www. nicksimper.net/darker-blue-interview/ [accessed Tuesday 8th February 2022].

19. How Ian Paice met Ritchie Blackmore. Ian Paice Drumtribe https://youtu. be/727rvc8J5Vc [accessed Tuesday 8th February 2022].

20. Academic Dictionaries and Encyclopedias https://en-academic.com/dic. nsf/enwiki/187548 [accessed Wednesday 9th February 2022].

21. Interview with Nick Simper. UKRockHistory https://youtu.be/ OtlDWVDDQxw [accessed Wednesday 9th February 2022]. Vanilla Fudge were, in fact, a highly experimental psychedelic rock band who did not always produce songs in the usual sense of the word. By the time Roundabout started to rehearse, they had released two albums, one of which 'The Beat Goes On' is particularly challenging to the norms of pop and rock, consisting of instrumental improvisations mixing music, narration and 'found' sounds. The influence on Deep Purple was somewhat indirect, being about general style and, perhaps, the lengthy improvisational passages that would become characteristic of early Mark II live performances. The use of organ on some Vanilla Fudge tracks is very reminiscent of Jon Lord's playing — certainly as it appeared on the Mark I albums and, indeed, *In Rock*.

22. There seems to be uncertainty about exactly how good a deal Lawrence got for the band. Keen to wet his own beak, he naturally took a small cut, but he always protested that the publishing deal that he negotiated for the band was unusually generous for the time.

5. Shades

1. Bloom, J. (2011). *Deep Purple Uncensored On The Record*. Coda Books Ltd.

2. That it was a good name for a band was proved by the fact that there had been two other, relatively local and short-lived, identically-titled combos active in the recent past. They, too, took their inspiration from the song.

3. Bloom, J. (2006). *Black Knight: Ritchie Blackmore*. Omnibus Press.

4. A Quiet Explosion: Deep Purple's 'Hush'. Writing on Music https://writingonmusic.com/2020/09/15/a-quiet-explosion-deep-purples-hush/ [accessed Thursday 10th February 2022].

5. Setlist.fm https://www.setlist.fm/setlist/deep-purple/1968/parkskolen-taastrup-denmark-13d89de1.html [accessed Thursday 10th February 2022].

6. Deep Purple Radio Special 1968-1976.

7. *Record Mirror*, September 1968.

8. Deep Purple: A Very Strange Case Indeed. *Melody Maker*, 14th September 1969.

9. UK Unknowns Score US Hit. *New Musical Express*, July 7th 1968.

10. Pure Luck Say Deep Purple. *New Musical Express*, September 14th 1968.

11. Tyler, K. On the Roundabout with Deep Purple. Deep Purple Appreciation Society http://www.deep-purple.net/archive/68-76history/roundabout.htm [accessed Saturday 12th February 2022]. In conversation with Jerry Bloom, Lord even said: 'Really I have to say that it was playing with Blackmore when he was at his height that still has a huge influence on me as a musician now.'

12. Ian Hansford interview with Jerry Bloom, 2nd November 2005.

13. Nick Simper website https://www.nicksimper.net/nicks-story/chapters-18-22/chapter-22-the-tv-debut-and-taliesyn/ [accessed Sunday 13th February 2022].

14. Ibid

15. Ibid

16. Peel, J. *The Book of Taliesyn. Disc & Music Echo*, June 7th 1969.

17. Deep Purple Appreciation Society http://www.deep-purple.net/review-files/inglewood/inglewood.htm [accessed Sunday 13th February 2022].

18. A number of TV appearances and promotional films featuring Mark I still exist. Nick Simper, on his website, has written of how the band's debut appearance was a now-lost live musical insert on David Frost's show. According to Simper, the performance was a little nervous, but the band got through it unscathed. Other than that, a moody film of the band performing 'Help!' can be found on YouTube — why it was made for a song that was never released as a single is a mystery. More bizarre is a proto-pop video of 'Hush'. Produced at some country estate or other, it becomes quickly apparent, upon watching it, that the only instruments available on

the day of filming were Blackmore's lead and Simper's bass guitars. Thus, an embarrassed-looking Lord mimes playing organ on top of a low wall, while Paice waves a couple of sticks around in imitation of drumming. For some reason, Evans sings wearing only a towel tied around his waist, as though he has recently stepped out of the shower. Even more weird is a film made by German television and based around the band's later track 'April'. Featuring truckloads of semi-nude young men, hard-hatted workers setting up chairs and music stands for an orchestra, as well as quite a bit of intrusive ambient noise, it is truly a one-off. The YouTube URL is given here so that the reader can 'enjoy' this oddity in full: https://youtu.be/CfZHISHvAvw

6.   Underground

1. Anderson, T. (2012). Still kissing their posters goodnight: Female fandom and the politics of popular music. Participations: Journal of Audience & Reception Studies, 9(2), 239-264.

2. Harrington, C. L. & Bielby, D. D. (2010). A life course perspective on fandom. International Journal of Cultural Studies, 13(5), 429-450.

3. Ridler, F. (nd). The 'fandom' phenomenon: How fan communities have evolved through the ages. Shorthand Social https://social.shorthand.com/FaithLRidler/32f52bNmNKu/the-fandom-phenomenon [accessed Monday 14th February 2022].

4. Ian Hansford interview with Jerry Bloom, 2nd November 2005.

5. Feldman-Barrett, C. (nd). The rise of Beatlemania. Museum of Youth Culture https://museumofyouthculture.com/beatlemania/ [accessed Monday 14th February 2022].

6. O'Sullivan, S. (2017). I saw the Beatles live, but no, I didn't scream. It's time to take female fans seriously. *The Washington Post*. May 26th 2017.

7. Sandvoss, C., Gray, J. & Harrington, C. L. (2017). Introduction: Why still study fans? In J. Gray, C. Sandvoss & C. L. Harrington (eds): Fandom. New York University Press.

8. Lacasa, P., De La Fuente, J., Garcia-Persia, M. & Cortes, S. (2017). Teenagers, fandom and identity. Persona Studies, 3(2), 51-65.

9. The Beatles banned segregated audiences, contract shows http://www.bbc.co.uk/news/entertainment-arts-14963752 [accessed Monday 14th February 2022].

10. Shukla, A. (2019). The Social Psychology of Heavy Metal & Rock Music: Research On Metalheads. Cognition Today https://cognitiontoday.com/the-social-psychology-of-heavy-metal-rock-music-research-on-metalheads/ [accessed Monday 14th February 2022].

11. *New Musical Express*, September 14th 1968.

12. Prince, T. (1970). Regal Report goes Deep Purple! *Fabulous 208* magazine, December 5th 1970.

13. Jon Lord Interview — Canadian TV 1969. Deep Purple Official https://youtu.be/AzgX8an7YHY [accessed Tuesday 15th February 2022].

14. Ibid

7. Changes

1. Derek Lawrence records early Purple and Jethro's toe. UKRockHistory https://youtu.be/BQ8QWCsMdyw [accessed Wednesday 16th February 2022].

2. Derek Lawrence discusses his involvement with Deep Purple management. Deep Purple Official https://youtu.be/p2UNVsX60LI [accessed Thursday 17th February 2022].

3. *New Musical Express*, February 22nd 1969.

4. *Deep Purple: A Critical Retrospective/Rock Review* [accessed Wednesday 16th February 2022].

5. This trend can be seen on, for example, the BBC sessions album released by the 1990s 'Britpop' band Elastica. Although they were only in existence for a relatively short period of time, the sessions that they recorded for the BBC give some excellent indications of how they were developing — and where they would have gone had they continued to operate. The BBC sessions for Elastica — as for Deep Purple and other bands — are a fascinating record of the songwriting process.

6. Nick Simper Interview with *Darker Than Blue* 1983 https://www.nicksimper.net/darker-blue-interview/ [accessed Thursday 17th February 2022].

7. *New Musical Express*, September 9th 1969.

8. *Melody Maker*, October 4th 1969.

9. Set list.fm https://www.setlist.fm/setlists/deep-purple-3bd6acc8.html?page=272 [accessed Saturday 19th February 2022].

10. *Melody Maker*, September 14th 1968

11. Ibid

12. Pure Luck say Deep Purple. *New Musical Express*, September 14th 1968.

13. Jon Lord interviewed for the *BBC Rock Family Trees* documentary on Deep Purple.

14. Nick Simper interviewed for the *BBC Rock Family Trees* documentary on Deep Purple.

15. In conversation with the author, 2017.

16. Gillan, I. (2016). *Ian Gillan: The Autobiography of Deep Purple's Lead Singer*. Music Press.

17. According to Gillan (in his autobiography, referenced above), these included putting in false teeth when doing a Bee Gees song. He drily comments that this was not well-received by every audience.

18. Gillan, I. (2016). *Ian Gillan: The Autobiography of Deep Purple's Lead Singer*. Music Press.

19. Ibid

20. Interview with Roger Glover, http://rockandrollgarage.com/roger-glover-recalls-how-he-joined-deep-purple-and-met-band-members/ [accessed Wednesday 23rd February 2022].

21. Roger Glover interviewed for the *BBC Rock Family Trees* documentary on Deep Purple.

22. Nick Simper interviewed for the *BBC Rock Family Trees* documentary on Deep Purple.

23. Jon Lord interview with Jerry Bloom, 21st November 2007.

24. Nick Simper Interview with *Darker Than Blue* 1983 https://www.nicksimper.net/darker-blue-interview/ [accessed Friday 25th February 2022]. The interview implies that, contrary to the 'lump sum' story, Simper took a slice of royalties after all, but only after a legal battle. It is a matter of record that such litigation occurred.

25. Jarvis, A. (2017). *Chasing Shadows: The Search for Rod Evans*. Wymer Publishing. This book was never intended to expose someone who clearly did not wish to be exposed, but to explore the mystery and use the outline idea of a 'quest' to find the missing singer as a way of thinking about what it means to be a Deep Purple fan. I was able to interview several people who had had contact with Evans since 1980, but none had been very recent and no one had a clue as to his current whereabouts. There is something rather admirable about someone who can so completely squash his own fame.

8. Concerto

1. When the music means something. *Melody Maker*, August 23rd 1969.

2. Ibid.

3. *New Musical Express*, September 13th 1969.

4. Thompson, D. (2003). *Smoke on the Water: The Deep Purple Story*. ECW Press. Lord appears to have much admired Emerson. On the Deep Purple Mark III live album *Live in London*, he introduces the various members of the band, giving his own name as 'Rick Emerson', perhaps a fictitious, but equally talented, brother of the ELP keyboardist — or perhaps a hybrid of Keith Emerson and that other keyboard maestro, Rick Wakeman. Either way, Lord is unduly modest in editing himself out of the 'genius keyboardist' conversation.

5. Blackmore would become an enthusiastic advocate of this approach. The title track of Rainbow's *Difficult to Cure* album is a rearrangement of part of Beethoven's Ninth Symphony. It would go on to find its way onto Deep Purple set lists during the early 1990s and, strangely, was performed during Ian Gillan solo concerts of the 2010s. Rainbow also recorded a rock version of Grieg's 'Hall of the Mountain King', although this was somewhat less successful.

6. The similarities between the two composers were perhaps further emphasised in 2007 when Lord wrote a *Durham Concerto*. Like the *Five Bridges Suite*, it sought to give a musical description of the titular town — which is geographically very close to Newcastle.

7. Stump, P. (1997). *The Music's All That Matters: A History of Progressive Rock*. Quartet Books Ltd.

8. Jon Lord, Deep Purple RAH London Symphony with Malcolm Arnold. MrDangermouse10 https://youtu.be/mzK19bzom0g [accessed Monday 28th February 2022].

9. Thompson, D. (2003). *Smoke on the Water: The Deep Purple Story*. ECW Press.

10. Jon Lord, Deep Purple RAH London Symphony with Malcolm Arnold. MrDangermouse10 https://youtu.be/mzK19bzom0g [accessed Tuesday 1st March 2022].

11. Malcolm Arnold: A Life. Classic fm, https://www.classicfm.com/composers/arnold/guides/malcolm-arnold-life/ [accessed Wednesday 2nd March 2022]

12. Jon Lord, Deep Purple RAH London Symphony with Malcolm Arnold. MrDangermouse10 https://youtu.be/mzK19bzom0g [accessed Tuesday 1st March 2022].

13. Jon Lord interview with Jerry Bloom, 21st November 2007.

14. Bloom, J. (2006). *Black Knight: Ritchie Blackmore*. Omnibus Press.

15. Thompson, D. (2003). *Smoke on the Water: The Deep Purple Story*. ECW Press.

16. Jeffries, N. (2016). Ritchie Blackmore: The Lost Interview. Classic Rock, June 10th 2016, https://www.loudersound.com/features/ritchie-blackmore-the-lost-interview [accessed Wednesday 2nd March 2022].

17. The lyrics as they stand are rather personal to Gillan — in some ways, problematically so. It is an interesting counter-factual to speculate on what the singer Lord would originally have had in mind — Rod Evans — would have come up with.

18. Thompson, D. (2003). *Smoke on the Water: The Deep Purple Story*. ECW Press.

19. Jon Lord interview from 2011 discussing his classical career. Deep Purple Official, https://youtu.be/W3ZsxRzwhsQ [accessed Thursday 3rd March 2022].

20. Bruce Dickinson discussing Jon Lord's *Concerto for Group and Orchestra* recording in May 2012. Deep Purple Official, https://youtu.be/CrHJN29o0VI [accessed Saturday 5th March 2022]. Dickinson, best known as the vocalist with heavy metal greats Iron Maiden, sang the second vocal part on the 2012 studio recording of the concerto — strangely, the first such recording in the concerto's — up to that point — long history.

21. Time Note: The *Concerto for Group and Orchestra*, https://timenote.info/en/events/The-Concerto-for-Group-and-Orchestra [accessed Saturday 5th March 2022].

22. Gillan, I. (2016). *Ian Gillan: The Autobiography of Deep Purple's Lead Singer*. Music Press.

23. Jon Lord — It's All Music TV Doc. Deep Purple Official, https://youtu.be/dr1-KaquogI [accessed Saturday 5th March 2022].

24. Jon Lord, Deep Purple RAH London Symphony with Malcolm Arnold. MrDangermouse10 https://youtu.be/mzK19bzom0g [accessed Saturday 5th March 2022].

25. Ibid. For those who may be interested, the exact word used by Arnold was the one beginning with 'c'. According to Lord, it caused one female member of the orchestra to storm out, necessitating apologies and general grovelling on the part of the conductor. The less-than-high-culture language certainly seems to have had the desired effect, however.

26. *Jon Lord — It's All Music* TV Doc. Deep Purple Official, https://youtu.be/dr1-KaquogI [accessed Monday 7th March 2022].

27. Jon Lord, Deep Purple RAH London Symphony with Malcolm Arnold. MrDangermouse10 https://youtu.be/mzK19bzom0g [accessed Sunday 6th March 2022].

28. *New Musical Express*, October 4th 1969.

29. Ibid.

30. *Melody Maker*, October 4th 1969.

31. Ibid.

32. Jon Lord + Ian Gillan on Concerto 1999 w/ Tommy Vance. JonLordorg, https://youtu.be/ZBy6O4VCoBQ [accessed Sunday 7th March 2022].

33. The Two Sides of Deep Purple.
     Melody Maker, November 1st 1969.

34. Rock Is Where We're At. *Record Mirror*, undated.

35. Purple Don't Think Classics are a Gas, Anymore.
     Disc magazine, October 3rd 1970.

36. Jon Lord interview with Jerry Bloom, 21st November 2007.

37. Jon Lord, Deep Purple RAH London Symphony with Malcolm Arnold.
     MrDangermouse10 https://youtu.be/mzK19bzom0g [accessed Monday
     7th March 2022].

9. Superstar

1. The full concert was finally released as a two CD set in 2002.

2. *Melody Maker*, December 20th 1969.

3. Purple at Hollywood Bowl with Philharmonic.
   New Musical Express, September 12th 1970.

4. Ibid.

5. Ibid.

6. Winston, K. (2018). The stormy, surprising history of *Jesus Christ Superstar*. *The Washington Post*, March 30th. The lyric in question asked whether 'Judas Iscariot / Had God on side'.

7. Karate, J. (2018). How it all began? The story of *Jesus Christ Superstar*. Broadway World, https://www.broadwayworld.com/article/The-Story-of-JESUS-CHRIST-SUPERSTAR-20180401 [accessed Friday 11th March 2022].

8. Sir Tim Rice provides a little insight into the genesis of *Jesus Christ Superstar*. Deep Purple Official, https://youtu.be/oAGOOaUq1tE [accessed Saturday 12th March 2022].

9. Ian Gillan — talks about 'Smoke on the Water', *Jesus Christ Superstar* & more — Radio broadcast 15/11/21. Raised on Radio, https://youtu.be/srH1AN0dZeM [accessed Saturday 12th March 2022].

10. Goodacre, M. (1999). Do you think you're what they say you are? Reflections on *Jesus Christ Superstar*. Journal of Religion and Film, 3(2).

11. Polkow, D. (nd). Andrew Lloyd Webber: From 'Superstar' to 'Requiem'. Religion Online, https://www.religion-online.org/article/andrew-lloyd-webber-from-superstar-to-requiem/ [accessed Saturday 12th March 2022].

12. 'Herod's Song' is something of a creative low point in the show, although it is always a crowd pleaser. Again, it does little to advance the plot and seems mainly to have been included as a way to give *Jesus Christ Superstar* its own 'Joseph'-style 'Pharaoh Moment'.

13. Sir Tim Rice provides a little insight into the genesis of Jesus Christ Superstar. Deep Purple Official, https://youtu.be/oAGOOaUq1tE [accessed Saturday 12th March 2022].

14. This was one of the reasons for the film version that finally emerged being so unsatisfactory. Ted Neeley, who plays Jesus, looks the part in many ways, but is too down-to-earth and ordinary for a character who the audience is told right at the start is exciting 'talk of God'. While he does not deserve the 'worst portrayal of Jesus on film ever' title accorded to him by the writers of the book, 'The Golden Turkey Awards', he can, with some justice, be described as less suitable for the role than its originator.

15. Ian Gillan — talks about 'Smoke on the Water', *Jesus Christ Superstar* & more — Radio broadcast 15/11/21. Raised on Radio, https://youtu.be/srH1AN0dZeM [accessed Sunday 13th March 2022].

16. Ibid.

17. Brin, D. (2014). Ian Gillan talks the different shades of Deep Purple. *The Jerusalem Post*, February 11th 2014.

18. Sir Tim Rice provides a little insight into the genesis of *Jesus Christ Superstar*. Deep Purple Official, https://youtu.be/oAGOOaUq1tE [accessed Sunday 13th March 2022].

19. Ibid.

20. On Deep Purple's ill-fated 1988 live release *Nobody's Perfect*, Gillan interrupts the rendition of 'Strange Kind of Woman' to give the audience an impromptu chorus of 'Superstar', which, ironically, is not sung by Jesus in the show, or on the original concept album.

10. Rock

1. *Disc* magazine, June 13th 1970.

2. *Melody Maker*, August 1970.

3. *New Musical Express*, February 1st 1971.

4. *New Musical Express*, June 6th 1970.

5. Official Charts, https://www.officialcharts.com/search/singles/black-night/ [accessed Saturday 19th March 2022].

6. *New Musical Express*, September 26th 1970.

7. Robinson, J. (2017). Deep Purple on 'Black Night': 'We thought the whole thing was a waste of time'. *Uncut* magazine, August 19th.

8. Ibid.

9. Deep Purple albums and songs sales. ChartMasters, https://chartmasters.org/2021/08/deep-purple-albums-and-songs-sales/ [accessed Saturday 19th March 2022].

10. Ibid.

11. Robinson, S. (1995). *Deep Purple In Rock Anniversary Edition*, CD Booklet.

12. Deep Purple Chart History, billboard.com, https://www.billboard.com/artist/deep-purple/chart-history/ats/ [accessed Saturday 19th March 2022].

13. *New Musical Express*, June 19th 1971.

14. The ordering of the tracks given here is that of current releases and, it seems, the original concert. Vinyl releases in the 1980s — presumably due to the time constraints of the format — rearranged the tracks to give a running order of 'Speed King' and 'Wring That Neck' on side one and 'Child in Time' and 'Mandrake Root' on side two.

15. Jon Lord interview with Jerry Bloom, 21st November 2007.

16. Robinson, S. (1995). *Deep Purple In Rock Anniversary Edition*, CD Booklet.

17. Bloom, J. (2011). *Deep Purple Uncensored On The Record*. Coda Books Ltd.

18. During planning sessions for the follow-up to the Mark III album *Stormbringer*, Blackmore suggested including a cover of 'Black Sheep of the Family', only to have the idea vetoed by the rest of the band. Rainbow were originally constituted with the limited ambition of putting out the cover as a solo single for Blackmore. He enjoyed the experience of recording it so much that he opted to simply leave Deep Purple and form a new band.

19. Bloom, J. (2006). *Black Knight: Ritchie Blackmore*. Omnibus Press.

20. Bloom, J. (2011). *Deep Purple Uncensored On The Record*. Coda Books Ltd.

21. Ian Gillan interview December 1970. Deep Purple Official, https://youtu.be/Gu_BPML6-qI [accessed Tuesday 22nd March 2022].

11. Today

1. Deep Purple *Come Taste The Band* Electronic Press Kit EPK. Deep Purple Official, https://youtu.be/6cEkqT5ljEA [accessed Tuesday 15th March 2022].

2. In fairness, *The House Of Blue Light* does contain one minor classic in the form of 'Mitzi Dupree', the song which gave the world the all-time great lyric, 'I knew right away that I'd seen her act before, in a room behind a kitchen in Bangkok and three or four times more in Singapore'.

3. The most obvious example of this comes on *Whoosh!* on which the brief instrumental 'Remission Possible' segues neatly into the album highlight 'Man Alive' in a way not unlike 'Fault Line' and 'The Painter' on *Deep Purple*.

4. Shukla, A. (2022). The Social Psychology Of Heavy Metal & Rock Music: Research On Metalheads. Cognition Today, https://cognitiontoday.com/the-social-psychology-of-heavy-metal-rock-music-research-on-metalheads/ [accessed Thursday 31st March 2022].

5. Sharman, L. & Dingle, G. A. (2015). Extreme metal music and anger processing. Frontiers in Human Neuroscience, 9.

6. Ritchie Blackmore Interview with Neil Jeffries, September 9th 1995.

About The Author

Adrian Jarvis is an academic and heavy rock fan. Of the former, if you put his name into the Internet, you are likely to be directed to scholarly articles on leadership; of the latter, Adrian has written a whole book, titled Chasing Shadows, detailing his Deep Purple obsession.

He travels widely and has lived in both Malaysia and Dubai (where he produced the present book). He is currently based in the north of England and works full-time in higher education.